3RD EDITION

FreeStuff
FOR
Quilters
ON THE
INTERNET

Judy Heim & Gloria Hansen

C&T PUBLISHING

Copyright © 2001 Judy Heim and Gloria Hansen

Developmental Editor: Barbara Kuhn
Copy Editor: Lucy Grijalva
Cover and Book Design: Christina Jarumay
Book Production: Nancy Koerner
Production Coordination: Diane Pedersen
Production Assistant: Jeff Carrillo

Library of Congress Cataloging-in-Publication Data

Heim, Judy.
        Free stuff for quilters on the Internet / Judy Heim and Gloria
Hansen.--3rd ed.
                p.   cm.
Includes bibliographical references and index.
        ISBN 1-57120-158-0 (paper trade)
1. Quilting--Computer network resources--Directories. 2.
Patchwork--Computer network resources--Directories. 3. Internet
addresses--Directories. 4. Web sites--Directories. 5. Free
material--Computer network resources--Directories. I. Hansen, Gloria.
II Title.
        TT835 .H3867 2001
        746.46′025--dc21

                                                2001002504

Published by C&T Publishing, Inc.
P.O. Box 1456
Lafayette, California 94549

Printed in China
10 9 8 7 6 5 4 3 2 1

DEDICATION

We dedicate this book to the spirit that inspires quilters and other craftspeople to share so freely of themselves, their skills, and their friendship on the Web. By sharing we open new worlds in the hearts and minds of others, including strangers we may never meet. We also grow friendships that are irreplaceable—well, like our own!

DEAR READER,

We assembled this third edition of Free Stuff for Quilters on the Internet by updating information for popular quilting Web sites that we recommended in earlier editions, as well as adding many new Web sites. We've also included lots of new tips on favorite things, such as fabric shopping on the Web and hunting for quilting patterns and tools through Web auctions. There are thousands of Web sites for quilters. You'll find patterns, advice, and camaraderie—in abundance. Sifting through them was a challenge. While we've tried to select the sites that we think offer the most valuable help for quilters, that doesn't mean there aren't many more out there that are equally illuminating and valuable. Also, because of the fluid nature of the Internet, it is inevitable that some of the Web sites in this book may have moved or even vanished. Had we included only those sites that are sure to be around for many moons from now, this book wouldn't be nearly as valuable. And, while you can find lots of free goodies on the Internet, you can learn more if you participate in quilting classes offered by your local quilt store. Quilt stores are excellent resources for quilting news, help, and advice. And they're just great places to meet other quilters, too!

—Judy and Gloria

SYMBOLS IN THIS BOOK

Web sites with the quilting bee icon host forums, E-mail lists, or bulletin boards where you can share information with other quilters.

This icon signifies a bit of Judy-and-Gloria hard-earned wisdom, or some valuable Internet tool that we've discovered.

When you see this icon, read carefully to avoid making one of the same silly mistakes we did!

This icon means that the Web site sells products that relate to the information on their site.

Table of Contents

why Quilters Love the Web!

Where do you go at 3 a.m. when you can't decide whether to use a cotton or a poly-blend batting? Who do you call when you can't find that recipe for tea-dyeing fabric and your favorite quilt store is closed? The Internet of course.

On the Web, quilting advice and camaraderie is always just a mouse click away. You can download free quilting patterns, find out what's hot in the art quilt world, tap into the Web sites of your favorite quilt magazines, learn how to repair and preserve your great grandmother's quilt, get help for machine quilting, plus hunt for out-of-print quilt patterns and books— all from the comfort of your family room, while lounging in your fuzzy robe and slippers.

Quilters and quilting advice are everywhere on the Web, because quilters are a chatty, sharing bunch. You'll be amazed at the quilt information you'll find in cyberspace, as well as the quilts you'll see and the quilters you'll meet.

We've put together this little guide to get you to all the handiest quilting information—and potential quilting friends—fast.

◆ THIS BOOK WILL GET YOU TO ANSWERS TO YOUR QUILTING QUESTIONS FASTER THAN ANYTHING ELSE WILL

You might say, "Why can't I just tap into a Web searcher like Altavista (**http://www.altavista.com**) to look for quilting patterns?" You can, but most of the information that the searcher will come up with will be meaningless product ads. Sifting them to find your answers will be a chore unto itself. We've done the work for you. We've sifted through thousands of quilting Web sites and organized the best into chapters that will speed you to quilting patterns, advice—and friends. With this book in hand you'll find:

- The biggest and best quilting Web sites where you'll find free patterns and lessons.
- Chat groups, Web discussion boards and other "cyber guilds" where quilters hang out.
- Web sites where you'll find answers to your questions about quilting techniques, as well as fabric, batting, thread, and other quilting products.
- Web sites where you can research quilt history—and visit museums with quilt collections—from the comfort of your computer.
- Web sites of quilting magazines, guilds, and societies.

◆ WEB BROWSER TIPS FOR QUILTERS

Whether you tap into the Web through an Internet service or America Online, the software centerpiece of your Web surfing is what's called a browser. In the old days you needed different sorts of software to do different things on the Net. For instance, you needed mail software to send and receive E-mail; a newsreader to read public discussions; you needed special software called FTP for "file transfer protocol" to download files to your computer. Plus you needed a browser to view (or browse through) the graphical portion of the Internet known as the Web. Now all those functions are built into browsers.

Most computers are sold with Netscape's Navigator or Microsoft's Internet Explorer already installed. You can also download them for free from **Netscape**'s Web site (**http://www.netscape.com**) or **Microsoft**'s (**http://www.microsoft.com**).

While you can use just about any computer to log onto the Internet in some fashion (even an original Apple II, circa 1979), to be able to view graphics you'll need a computer manufactured in at least the last 8 years. If you have an older computer, download a copy of the **$35 Opera** browser (**http://www.operasoftware.com**) which will run on any Windows 3.x-running PCs as old as 386SX's with 6 megabytes of RAM.

If you're running an older Macintosh, head to **Chris Adams's Web Browsers for Antique Macs** web page (**http://www.edprint.demon.co.uk/se/macweb.html**) and download Tradewave's MacWeb or an early version of NCSA Mosaic.

If you've never configured Internet software before, you'll need someone to help you, even if you're a computer genius (believe us, we know). Your ISP will (or should) give you directions on how to set up a Windows system or a Macintosh to at least log on to their service.

But once you're connected, you're pretty much on your own.

That's why we've put together this little tutorial.

T I P

If You Can't Access a Web Page Try These Tricks:

• If Netscape's logo keeps "snowing" but doesn't display any page, it may be because Netscape has frozen. Try accessing the Web site with Explorer instead. For convenience, cut the URL from Netscape's Location bar and past it into Explorer's.

• If you click on a highlighted link on a Web page but you don't get anything, try right-clicking on the link instead. From the pop-up box select "Open in New Window" or "Open Frame In New Window."

• If you click to a Web page with Netscape and the Web page appears to be blank, try accessing it with Explorer instead. Netscape is fussy about certain types of coding on pages and may refuse to load a page because it choked on some bit of coding.

• If a page doesn't appear to load properly, click the **Reload** button.

• If you're running Internet Explorer 5 and occasionally Web pages load only partially, you need to download a patch from Microsoft's Web site (**http://www.microsoft.com**).

HOW TO TAP INTO A WEB PAGE

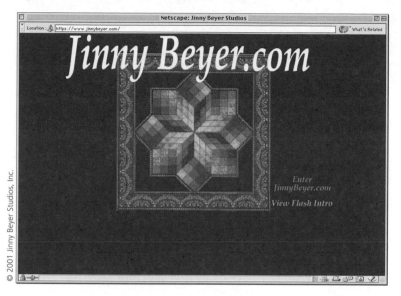

To get to a Web page, such as Jinny Beyer's, type its address, also known as its URL, or Universal Resource Locator—**http://www.jinnybeyer.com**—into the **Address:** bar in Internet Explorer, or the **Location:** bar in Netscape. In newer browsers you can type simply **www.jinnybeyer.com** or even **jinnybeyer**.

Take note that the case of the letters is important.

You can also cut and paste URLs from other documents into the address or location bar. (Highlight the address with your mouse, press **Ctrl-C** or **⌘-C** on a Mac, then place the mouse in the location bar and press **Ctrl-V** or **⌘-V** on a Mac to paste it in. Then hit <Enter>.)

To move to other pages in the Web site, click on high-lighted words, or, whenever your mouse cursor changes into a hand when it's positioned on an object, click your mouse to go there.

What does all that gobbledygook in a URL mean?

The **http:** tells your Internet service what kind of document you are trying to access on the Internet. HTTP stands for "hyper-text transfer protocol," the protocol of the Web. You might run into **ftp:** which stands for "file transfer protocol," an early Internet scheme for transferring files. The protocol is always followed by **//** which separates it from the document's address.

Next comes the domain name. For example, **www.ctpub.com**. The triple-w designates C&T's Web subdirectory on its Internet server. The **.com** suffix indicates that C&T is a commercial entity. If C&T were a university it would have an **.edu** suffix or an **.org** one if it were a non-profit. The words that follow the domain name, separated by slashes, designate further subdirectories. Many, though not all, URLs end with a specific file name.

**How to Locate a Web Site
if It Appears to Have Vanished**

Sometimes when you type a Web page's address into your browser, the browser (or the Web) will spit back some gobbledy-gook error message. Here's a trick: try working back through the URL as if it were a directory address on your computer. For example, on Jinny Beyer's Web site you can find a free "rose" quilt pattern at:
http://www.jinnybeyer.com/blocks/block29.html

If the pattern doesn't appear when you type this into your browser, trying going backward one "step" to:
http://www.jinnybeyer.com/blocks

If there's nothing there, or if you get a weird error message, try going back to the main domain name at:
http://www.jinnybeyer.com

If there's nothing at the main domain name, then it's time to head to a searcher like **Excite** (**http://www.excite.com**) and try typing "Jinny Beyer" or, for more specific hits, "Jinny Beyer quilts" to see if the searcher comes up with the new domain name. That's merely an example, for Jinny's Web site is of course at her domain name.

Index of /msue/imp/mod03

Name	Last modified	Size	Description
Parent Directory	20-Sep-99 15:23	-	
01700001.html	05-Aug-99 16:36	3k	
01700002.html	05-Aug-99 16:36	2k	
01700003.html	05-Aug-99 16:36	3k	
01700004.html	05-Aug-99 16:36	2k	
01700005.html	05-Aug-99 16:36	2k	
01700006.html	05-Aug-99 16:36	2k	
01700007.html	05-Aug-99 16:36	2k	
01700008.html	05-Aug-99 16:36	2k	
01700009.html	05-Aug-99 16:36	2k	
01700010.html	05-Aug-99 16:37	2k	
01700011.html	05-Aug-99 16:37	2k	
01700012.html	05-Aug-99 16:37	2k	

If you're working back through a URL and get a directory that lists files like this, you can click on the highlighted names to view or even download them. If you see a file with an "HTM" or "HTML" at the end of its name, click on it. That's a Web page document. If it has a .GIF or .JPG extension that's a picture. If you get an error message like "Access denied," try going further back through the URL. This is a directory for the Web site of the **Michigan State University Extension** *(***http://www.msue.msu.edu***) where you can find all sorts of pamphlets on home-related topics.*

◆ COMMON ERROR MESSAGES WHEN YOU ENTER A WEB ADDRESS

✋ *404 Not Found*
The requested URL /blocks/tips.html was not found on this server.

Reason: Your browser was able to find the Internet service or the computer on which the Web site was or is hosted, but no such page was found on the service. (The very last "word" at the end of the URL is the page's file name or address. For example tips.html.) Maybe the Web site owner removed that particular page. Or perhaps the Web site no longer exists.

Fix: Try working back through the URL as explained in the previous tip, to see if you can locate the Web site, or determine if the site itself is gone from the service. Also, try suffixing the page's address with "htm" or "html" instead of its current extension. For example, in place of **tips.html** type **tips.htm**. (An HTML suffix is the same as an HTM, but some Web page hosting services require that Web pages be named with one or the other. Typing the wrong extension is a common mistake.)

✋ *DNS Lookup Failure*
or
Unable to locate the server. The server does not have a DNS entry.

Reason: DNS stands for "domain name server." A domain name is the first part of a URL—for instance, in **www.ctpub.com**, **ctpub.com** is the domain name. Every Internet service (and AOL) has a database of such Web page host addresses. When you type a URL, the first thing your browser does is tell your Internet service to look up the domain name in its database, to find out where it's located. If it can't find it, your Internet service's computer may poll other domain name directories around the Internet to determine if any of them know where the domain name can be found. If none of them do, you may get the error message "DNS Lookup Failure."

Why can't they find the domain name? Maybe it no longer exists. Or perhaps it's so new that the domain name databases your Internet service uses can't find it. Sometimes you also get this error message when there's heavy traffic on the Internet. Your Internet service is taking too long to look up the name, so your browser errors out.

Fix: Try typing the URL into your browser later in the day. If you still get the error message, try the URL a few days, or even a week later. If you still get error messages the domain name no longer exists.

✋ No Response from Server

Reason: Your browser is unable to get a timely response from the Web site's host computer. This can be because of heavy traffic on the Internet, or on the branch of the Internet you are traveling. It can be because the computer that's hosting the Web site is overloaded (everyone is tapping in). Or it can be because your Internet service is overloaded, or its own computers are experiencing slowdowns for technical reasons.

Fix: Try the URL either in a few minutes, or later in the day.

✋ Server Is Busy

Reason: A common error message issued by heavily trafficked Web sites, it means that too many people are trying to tap in.

Fix: Try accessing the Web site later.

◆ HOW TO BOOKMARK QUILTING ADVICE

Web browsers let you "bookmark" sites so that you can visit them later by simply fishing through your bookmark catalog. You usually just click a bookmark icon (or Favorites in Internet Explorer) or select the feature from a toolbar to add to your bookmark list the Web site that you're currently visiting.

You Can Add Shortcuts to Web Sites on Your Windows or Macintosh Desktop.

Say there's a particular Web site you like to visit every day. If you're running Windows 95/98 or a Macintosh you can add a shortcut to it from your desktop. When you click on the shortcut your browser will load, dial your Internet service, and speed you to the Web site. Use your mouse to drag the site's URL from a link in a Web page. Or, if you're using Internet Explorer, drag from the Address bar to the left of the Links bar or the Favorites menu. If you're using Netscape, drag the icon to the left of Location: when a page is loaded. Your mouse cursor should change into a circle with a slash as you drag the URL to the desktop.

Adding Shortcuts In Netscape

Create buttons on your personal toolbar in Netscape to whiz you to Web sites you visit frequently. First, display the toolbar by pulling down the View menu, selecting Show, and placing a check beside Personal Toolbar.

American Quilter's Society Online - Netscape

File   Edit   View   Go   Communicator   Help

Back   Forward   Reload   Home   Search   Netscape

Bookmarks   Location: http://www.aqsquilt.com/

While the Web page is displayed, drag the Location icon to the Personal Toolbar just below.

American Quilter's Society Online - Netscape

File   Edit   View   Go   Communicator   Help

Back   Forward   Reload   Home   Search   Netscape

Bookmarks   Location: http://www.aqsquilt.com/

The icon should look like this when you're successfully dragging the Web site's location to your toolbar.

American Quilter's Society Online - Netscape

File   Edit   View   Go   Communicator   Help

Back   Forward   Reload   Home   Search   Netscape

Bookmarks   Location: http://www.aqsquilt.com/

American Quilte

American Quilter's Society Online

Click this button whenever you want your browser to take you to the Web site of the American Quilter's Society.

TIP

While a Web page is displayed, right-click on the page and from the pop-up menu select *Add Bookmark*.

Adding Shortcuts in Explorer

*To add a bookmark
to Explorer click
Favorites/Add to
Favorites.*

*You can also drag
URLs to the Links
toolbar to create
buttons. Display
the Links toolbar by
heading to View/
Toolbars/Links.*

*The icon should
look like this when
you're successfully
dragging the Web
site's location to
your toolbar.*

*Click this button
whenever you
want Explorer to
take you to the
Web site of the
American Quilter's
Society.*

You Can Customize Your Browser's Personal Toolbar by Adding Bookmarks.

You can customize the personal toolbar in **Communicator**, or the Links bar in **Internet Explorer** by adding not only icons for frequently visited URLS, but folders of bookmarks. In Communicator add a URL to the personal toolbar by dragging a link from a Web page or by dragging the icon to the left of **Location:** when a page is loaded. To add a folder instead to the personal toolbar click the Bookmarks icon, select **Edit Bookmarks** and highlight the folder you wish to place on the toolbar. Right-click and select **Set as Toolbar Folder**. In Internet Explorer you can similarly customize the Links bar by adding individual URLs as well as folders. Drag folders from the **Favorites** menu to add them to the **Links** bar. To add a URL to the link bar drag it from the **Address** bar to the left of the Links bar, from the **Favorites** menu or from a Web page.

You Can Use Third-Party Bookmark Software to Organize Your Bookmarks.

There are a lot of low-cost utilities for organizing bookmarks that you can download from the Web. These are particularly handy if you're using two browsers—both Netscape and Internet Explorer for example. They enable you to store your bookmarks in a central location, and organize them into folders with icons—and in a more efficient manner than you can in your browser. Some utilities also let you password-protect bookmarks. A good spot to download them is **C/net's Shareware.Com** (**http://www.shareware.com**). Search for the phrase "bookmark organizer." For PCs one we like is **LinkMan Professional** from Thomas Reimann. For Macs we like **URL Manager Pro**, the shareware program from **Alco Blom** (**http://www.url-manager.com**).

◆ HOW TO FIND YOUR WAY AROUND QUILTING WEB SITES WITHOUT GETTING LOST

• Click the **Back** button in your browser to return to previously visited Web sites. Right-click on the **Back** button in your browser for a list of Web sites you've recently visited. Click on their names to return to them.

• Click the **History** button or select the history feature from a drop-down menu to list previously visited URLs.

• Click your browser's drop-down location box, which displays the last dozen or so URLs that you have actually typed into the browser (in other words, it doesn't display links that you've clicked on something to get to).

◆ COOL TRICKS FOR PRINTING & SAVING WEB PAGES WITH QUILTING PATTERNS

You're probably going to want to print quilting patterns or advice you find on the Web. Here are some tips to make your life easier when you do it:

How To Print an Entire Web Page

From your browser's menu select **Print**. If the page has frames you may need to first click on the frame that you want to print in order to select it. From the File menu select **Page Setup** if you want to print the URL or date on the page (this feature is available only in newer browsers).

How to Save a Picture on a Web Page

Images on Web pages are copyrighted just as text is. If you want to use them in any way—either to print to distribute to your friends or post on your own Web pages—the same rules apply as to text: you need to ask the owner's permission first!

Position your cursor over the image and right-click. On a Mac click-hold. A menu box will pop up. Select **Save Image As...** or **Save Picture As...**

You can later view it in either your browser or a graphics program like Paint Shop Pro. You can even import it into a word processing document. (In Microsoft Word, from the Insert menu select Picture.)

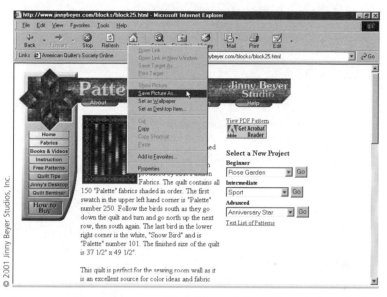

Say you want to save a copy of the picture of the quilt made from the free "Snow Bird" quilt pattern found on Jinny Beyer's Web site. Right click on it in Windows or click-hold on a Mac and select Save as... (Remember that pictures on Web pages are copyrighted by their artist and you should not print or distribute them without asking permission first.)

Remember, Web Pages Are Copyrighted—and So Are the Free Quilting Patterns on Them! Web pages are copyrighted just as any publication is. Or any needlework design, for that matter. You should not print them except for your own personal use without asking permission from the Web page's owner. The same holds true for any elements on the page, including text, but also graphics. Never, ever print or distribute these things— or, heaven forbid, put them on your own Web page.

TIP

In Explorer, if you right-click on a Web page, up pops a menu containing an option for printing the page.

How to Save an Entire Web Page to Disk

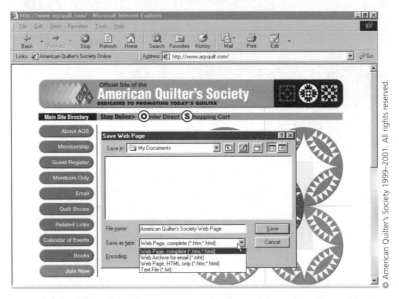

*You can use the **File/Save As** command in your browser to save a Web page either in full, or save only the text. Depending upon your browser, how the Web page can be saved—and how it will appear when you try to redisplay it will differ. To view the page once you've saved it, use your browser's **File/Open** command. Click the **Browse** button to browse to the directory where you saved the page (you do remember, right?).*

The easiest way to save Web pages is to use a Web-page saving utility. For Windows-running PCs, our favorite is **SurfSaver** (**http://www.surfsaver.com**) from askSam Systems. You can download a free version from the Web site, or pony up $30 for the advertising-free version.

For the Mac, we like **Web Devil** (**http://www.chaoticsoft ware.com**) from Chaotic Software. It will save Web pages with all the images, links and scripts intact. You can download and try it for 15 days, or buy it for $35.

◆ MORE TIPS ON SAVING AND PRINTING QUILTING PATTERNS FOUND ON WEB PAGES

Some Web sites, like Jinny Beyer's, give you the option of displaying and printing a quilting pattern in any of several different ways:

1. You can display it on a Web page. In that case you can save or print the page just as you would any other Web page.

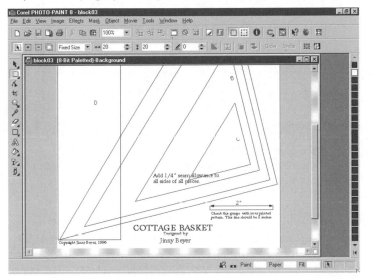

Some quilting Web sites such as Jinny Beyer's offer free patterns in common graphics formats like TIF. You'll need to use a graphics program like Corel Photopaint to view them once you save them to disk.

2. You can download the pattern in a common graphics file format. Typical formats are TIF, PCX, and BMP. There might either be a download button that you click, or the Web page will display the pattern as a graphic. You would right-click on it, or click-hold on a Mac to save it to disk. Be sure to remember its file name so that you can find it. Once you've saved the pattern to disk you will need to use a graphics program like **Paint Shop Pro** (**http://www.jasc.com**) or Photoshop to view it. Depending upon the file format you might even be able to display it in Windows Paint or your word processor. You can print it with these programs. You can also shrink or enlarge the pattern if necessary.

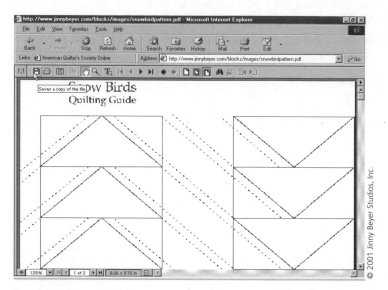

To print or save a quilting pattern stored in PDF or Acrobat format, you will need to click the appropriate buttons in the Acrobat viewer instead of using the print feature in your Web browser.

3. You can display and print it in Acrobat format. Some quilting Web sites post their patterns in the popular desktop publishing format called PDF for "portable document format." (Many government agencies also post documents in this format.) In order to display these files you'll need to download and install the free Acrobat reader from **Adobe Systems** (**http://www.adobe.com**). Once you install it, whenever your Web browser encounters a PDF file on a Web page, it will automatically fire up Acrobat and display the document for you. To save or print the pattern, you'll need to click the appropriate buttons in the Acrobat screen.

✋ *Note:* Be sure to test print a pattern and measure its dimensions carefully. Variations in printers may cause some printers to print quilting patterns with slightly askew dimensions.

◆ MINI-TUTORIAL ON HOW TO SAVE AND ENLARGE A QUILTING PATTERN FROM A WEB SITE

You'll find patterns stored in common graphics formats like JPG, BMP, or TIF on many quilting Web sites. Here's what to do with them.

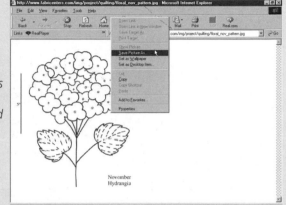

To save a quilting pattern to disk, right-click on it in Windows or click-hold on a Mac and select **Save as...** *In order for the proper menu to pop up, you must place your cursor directly over the image. This floral applique pattern, which can be found on the Web site of Jo-Ann Fabrics, is in JPEG format. When you save it to disk it will be stored with a .JPG extension.*

According to the directions on Jo-Ann's Web site you need to enlarge this image by 200 percent in order to use it as a quilting pattern. To do that, display the pattern in a graphics program. Pull up the image resize menu and increase both its width and its height by 200 percent. You can now print the pattern, or save it with a new file name. To print it use the graphics program's File/Print feature.

◆ TIPS FOR CUTTING PRINTING TIME & SAVING ON INKJET CARTRIDGES

If you don't want to print a Web page's background... In your browser, click **File/Page Setup**. A dialog box will appear. In it you can instruct your browser not to print the background.

Lower your printer's print quality... How you do this will depend upon your printer. In most cases, you'd click **File/Print** in your browser, then click **File/Print** then click the **File Properties** button. Head to the Graphics tab if there's one.

If a Web page has frames... In other words, if looks as if it's divided up into boxes, print only the frame that contains the information you want. Click on the frame to select it. In your browser click **File/Print Frame**.

Surf and print without pictures... You can tell your browser not to display the pictures on a Web page. This is helpful if you wish to print only the text on a Web page—to save on those pricey inkjet cartridges, or to save time. In newer versions of Netscape, click **Edit/Preferences**, then head to the **Advanced** category. Remove the check in the box beside **Automatically Load Images**. Click **OK**. In newer versions of Explorer, click **Tools/Internet Options**. Head to the **Advanced Tab** and under Multimedia, remove the check beside "Show

Pictures." Scroll farther down. Under **Printing**, remove the check beside "Print Background Colors and Images." Click **OK** to make the changes permanent.

TIP If you attempt to print a Web page, and the portion that you wish to print doesn't print, it may be because you haven't selected the proper frame on the Web page. Click on the part of the page that you want to print, then try printing it again.

TIP **Set Up Internet Explorer to Print Large Print Pages—and Make Web Pages Easier to Read.** Do some Web sites make you squint, with their flashing backgrounds and teeny print? You can set up more recent versions of Microsoft's Explorer browser to display Web pages in bigger, more easily readable type—and also to print pages in bigger print. You can also set the browser to turn off those annoying Web page backgrounds.

Head to **Tools/Internet Options**. Under the **General** tab, click the **Accessibility** button. A dialog box will appear in which you can set the browser to ignore colors, fonts and font sizes on Web pages. When you select these options, Explorer will use the fonts and colors you've set as the default on your system. Or, you can set them specifically for the browser by heading back to the **General** tab. Click the **Colors** and **Fonts** buttons to set up the browser's display. Click **OK** when you're finished making your selections.

To get rid of Web page backgrounds when you go to print, click **Tools/Internet Options**. Head to the **Advanced Tab** and under **Printing**, remove the check beside "Print Background Colors and Images." Click **OK** to make the changes permanent.

Netscape offers some features to set your own fonts and colors, but they don't work very well. If you have vision problems, we recommend using Explorer instead.

◈ HOW TO DOWNLOAD QUILTING SOFTWARE FROM THE INTERNET

In most instances all you need to do is mouse-click on the highlighted name of the program or file on a Web page and your browser will start downloading—hopefully by prompting you where you want to store the file.

But sometimes that doesn't work. If that happens, right-click in Windows or click-hold on a Mac on the name of the file. When a pop-up menu appears, click on Save Link As... and the browser will begin downloading.

*You can download from the Web site of **Quilt-Pro Systems** (**http://www.quiltpro.com**) demos of the company's quilt design software for PCs and Macs, including the company's flagship quilt design software Quilt-Pro 2 as well as Quilt 1-2-3. In most instances all you need to do is click on a highlighted program or file name in order to download it.*

> **TIP**
>
> As a file download starts, always check that the file is writing itself to your disk with the same name as its stored on the remote computer, so you know what to do with it.

Once you click on the file name your browser will ask you where on your computer you want to store the software. Once you select a directory, click Save.

Once the file begins transferring, this box will pop up, showing you the progress of the download.

◆ JUDY & GLORIA'S TEN-STEP PROGRAM FOR FIXING BROWSER AND GRAPHICS CRASHES

After you spend an hour or so clicking around Web sites your browser may start acting flaky. Maybe Web pages stop appearing quickly or your computer grinds its disk a lot. Maybe your PC just locks up. Any number of things could be causing the problem. Follow these steps to make your life browser-crash-free:

Step 1. Cold boot the PC. In other words, shut down your software, turn the power off, and turn it back on a few minutes later when the disk stops spinning. That will clean any flotsam out of its memory. Your browser will be flying again when you log back on the Web, but this solution is only temporary. Some people reboot their PC several times in the course of an evening. We think that's unnecessary. That's why we recommend the next steps.

Step 2. Head to the Web sites of the maker of your PC, its video card and its modem and download any fixes or new drivers.

Step 3. Clean up your hard disk by running **Scandisk** and **Disk Defragmenter**. Click **Start/Programs/ Accessories/System Tools**. (You should do this every few weeks.)

Step 4. If you're running Windows 95/98/2000 head to Microsoft's Web site (**http://www.microsoft.com**) and download any new fixes, patches, or upgrades. (There are always fixes to download for Windows.) While you're there, download the current version of Internet Explorer and any fixes for that too, if that's the browser you run. If you use Netscape, get the newest one of that (**http://www.netscape.com**).

Step 5. If you're running a version of AOL 3.0 earlier than 131.75, you need to upgrade. For AOL 4.0, upgrade if it's lower than 134.224. If you're running Windows 95 and experiencing crashes with AOL 5.0 or 4.0 you might want to return to using AOL 3.0. Use the keyword "upgrade." To find out what version of AOL you're running click **Help/About America Online**. Hit **Ctrl-R** when the AOL window pops up.

Step 6. A surfing browser will push your computer's memory to the limit. Try shutting down unnecessary applications while surfing and see if that helps. Press **Ctrl-Alt-Delete** to get a list of applications and close down everything but Explorer, Systray, and your browser. To troubleshoot your system further, right-click on **My Computer** and choose **Properties**. In the **Device Manager** tab make sure that no red or yellow flags signal hardware conflicts. In the **Performance** tab make sure that System Resources scores at least 85% free. Click the **Virtual Memory** button and select "Let Windows manage my virtual memory settings." Click **OK**. If AOL's crashing you should try shutting down your virus software to see if that might be the source of the conflict.

Step 7. Your browser needs lots of disk space for caching. At least 50 megabytes, or 10 percent of your disk should be free. You should empty your browser's cache weekly. Delete Netscape's history file (netscape.hst) and Cache folder. Clean out AOL's cache by heading to **My AOL/Preferences/WWW**. Head to the **General** tab and click the **Delete Files** and **Clear History** buttons. For Explorer delete the folder **Temporary Internet Files** found in the Windows directory.

Step 8. If Web page pictures look smeary or if your computer locks up while you're scrolling down a page, your video driver or graphics card may be at fault. Right-click on an empty spot in the desktop, and click **Properties**. In the **Settings** tab change the **Colors** to 256. Click **Apply**.

Under the Performance tab move down the Hardware Acceleration slider a notch. Click **OK**.

Step 9. If your browser crashes while printing Web pages it may be because your printer needs an updated driver. Or, it might need a bidirectional cable. Most printers are sold with bidirectional cables these days, but there's always that odd duck. But try this first: head to the **Control Panel**, click the **Printer** icon, and right-click on the icon for your printer. Select **Properties**. In the Details tab select **Spool Settings**. Set **Print** direct to printer. If there's an option to disable bi-directional support, do it.

Step 10. If you think Netscape is at fault head to Netscape's crash troubleshooting page (**http://help.netscape.com/kb/client/970203-1.html**). If you think Explorer is at fault, write down the **Invalid Page Fault** error message it spits out then search for the message on Microsoft's tech support site (**http://www.microsoft.com/support**). Better yet, search for the names of your computer, your graphics card, and your modem on both Web sites. The chances are very good that you'll find your solution on one of them.

Here are more things to try:

If you're feeling ambitious download a new version of your browser, then uninstall your old one (this step is important). Then reinstall the new one.

If Explorer spits out a Java or ActiveX error while trying to display a Web site, then it goes belly up, try disabling these scripting languages. From the **Tools** menu select **Internet Options**. Head to the **Security** tab and click the **Internet** icon. Click dots beside **Disable** in these categories: Download signed ActiveX controls; Run ActiveX controls and plugins; Active Scripting; and Scripting of Java applets. Under Java select **Disable Java**.

If AOL is the source of your woes (the sign that the problem lies with your AOL software and not with too many people logging on to the AOL network is that AOL freezes without the hourglass symbol), try deleting the AOL Adapter. From the **Start** menu select **Settings**, then **Control Panel**. Click the **Network** icon and head to the **Configuration** tab. Highlight "AOL Adapter" and click Remove. Restart Windows. Sign back on to AOL and AOL will reinstall an updated version of the adapter.

Try calling a different AOL number and see if that remedies the freeze-ups. Head to My AOL/Access Numbers to find a new number.

Use the keywords "help community" to find up-to-date solutions to AOL freeze-ups.

Say you can't get your browser to download software in a sane fashion. Maybe it spits kooky characters across the screen when you try. There's a simple way out: right-click in Windows or click-hold on a Mac on the file name until a menu box pops up. Select **Save Link As...** and you'll be on your way.

One thing to keep in mind is that if the file transfer progress box flashes on your screen, then disappears, your browser may not have saved the file. That will be because it's not tapped into the correct Web page to actually download the file. You should be on the Web page that displays the highlighted file name, or a "Download now" link. In other words, you need to be only one mouse click away from the file download in order to get this to work.

◆ HOW TO FIND PATTERNS, PEOPLE, PRODUCTS, AND MORE!

Looking for help with your Pfaff? How about that pal you shared a sewing machine with in high school? To quickly find what, or whom you're looking for on the Internet all you need to do is head to one of these big search engines:

EXCITE
http://www.excite.com

SNAP.COM
http://www.snap.com

DOGPILE
http://www.dogpile.com

WHOWHERE? PEOPLE FINDER
http://www.whowhere.lycos.com

SWITCHBOARD PEOPLE FINDER
http://www.switchboard.com

Type the name of the pattern or person you're looking for—or even the name of a recipe or rare disease—and the searcher will come up with a list of possibly applicable Web sites or directory hits. Usually you can find at least one information-chocked Web site within the first two "pages" of matches. From that page you can scuttle around the Web, to related links and Web pages.

Should the file transfer progress box shown on page 27 disappear, don't panic. Its disappearance does not mean that your computer has stopped downloading the file. For instance, sometimes it disappears if you click on something else on the Web page or in your browser. You will probably find the transfer box tucked away in some other corner of your computer screen (like the bottom program status bar) and the transfer still faithfully chugging away in the background.

◆ THINKING OF BARGAIN HUNTING FOR QUILT TOPS, VINTAGE BLOCKS AND PATTERNS IN WEB FLEA MARKETS? READ OUR TIPS FIRST!

Web flea markets are fantastic places to shop for old quilt tops, vintage blocks, old patterns and books—even missing pieces and a manual for that Singer featherweight. Our favorite cyber-flea marketing spot is **eBay** (**http://www.ebay.com**). Here are some general shopping tips to help you:

- **How safe is buying from Web flea markets?** It depends *a lot* on what you're buying—in our opinion. High-ticket items like consumer electronics are high risk. Remember that in most instances you're not actually buying from the flea market but from individuals who advertise on it. Your entire transaction will probably be with a stranger about whom you know nothing but an E-mail address. Judy often buys vintage patterns, beads, and laces on eBay, but rarely buys anything over $10. She frankly isn't too worried that someone who sells old buttons will turn out to be a con artist. She would *never* buy computer equipment from these sites.

- **Before you bid, check the seller's buyer ratings.** Web auction sites let buyers post comments about sellers after a transaction. Although these "buyer ratings" are often not what they're cracked up to be—they can be easily forged, and aggrieved buyers may be too timid to post "negative feedback"—if a seller boasts hundreds of happy customers, that can be a good sign that they may in fact send you your 99 cent buttons without laundering your check.

- **Never send money orders.** Some sellers accept only money orders. If you send a money order you have no way of knowing that your money actually arrived in their hands and they cashed the check.

- **Check the "Ending Today" listings for the best buys.** Most people bid on items in the last hours—or even the last minute before an auction ends. (People who do their bidding in the last minute are called "snipers.")

• **Ask questions before bidding.** Never take anything for granted. If the seller maintains in their description that "all pattern pieces are intact" ask them how they know. Did they actually take them out of the package and count them? Does the package appear to have been opened? Are the instructions in one piece? Does that "Victorian lace" come with a "poly blend" tag? Find out what they plan to charge for shipping.

• Use the auction site's search engine if you're shopping for something specific. If you're looking for something particular, like poodle-themed embroidery patterns from the '50s (Judy has a collection of those accumulated from eBay), search the entire auction site for different words, combinations of words, and shortened forms of words, and even misspellings. For instance—poodle, podle, emb., poodle pat.—will all turn up patterns with the proper qualifications. We've found quilt tops accidentally posted with the Rolex watches this way.

• **Save all correspondence with the seller.** Keep the URL of the Web page where the item appears. And keep in mind, before you bid, that if you get ripped off you'll have little if any recourse.

• **If you're buying a pricey item, use an escrow service.** An escrow service will act as a middle-man in the transaction. You send the check to the escrow service. The seller sends you the item. When you inform the service that you've received the item satisfactorily, the service forwards your check on to the seller. Some of the online auction sites offer this service for a modest fee. Keep in mind that not all sellers will agree to use an escrow service, so be sure to ask about it before bidding.

CHAPTER 2

how to Find Quilting Patterns, Friends & Fun on America Online

A merica Online hosts some wonderful quilting and craft forums where you'll find lots of free patterns to download, fabric swaps to join, and of course many other quilters with whom to chat. On AOL you can chat with quilters both on forum bulletin boards and through special quilting chat rooms. AOL also hosts Web pages for many quilters and quilting stores. The service has a few idiosyncrasies though, and that's why we've put together this little guide to speed you on your way to the quilting fun on AOL.

AMERICA ONLINE IS A GOOD PLACE TO GET STARTED IF YOU'VE NEVER BEEN ONLINE BEFORE

AOL is a great way to get started on the Internet if you've never tapped into cyberspace before.

You can get a free AOL startup disk by calling (800)-827-6364, or have a friend download the software for you from **America Online**'s Web site (**http://www.aol.com**).

> **TIP**
>
> *Having Problems with Your America Online Connection?*
>
> Head to the **Members Helping Members** forum on America Online for the best tech support on the service. Type the keywords "help community" in the location bar at the top of the screen to get there. This will take you to a public discussion area where you're sure to find other members who are having the same problem as you are—or who know the solution.

Among AOL's disadvantages are its hourly fees to access some areas of the service and the fact that the service's access numbers are long-distance calls for some. Also, AOL's numbers are sometimes busy in the evening (when all the kids are online). AOL also charges additional hourly access fees for anyone connecting from outside the continental United States or anyone calling through an AOL 800 number.

✋ Warning!

Very often it happens that when you click on a menu choice in a quilting or craft forum on America Online you find yourself jettisoned out onto the Internet and thrashing around somebody's retail Web site (where it is hoped you will buy something). That's one of the unfortunate aspects of AOL. Sometimes it's hard to tell when you're on the Internet and when you're on AOL. Often the only way to tell that you've landed on the Internet is that AOL's weird and quirky little built-in Web browser with "World Wide Web" at the top of the screen pops up. To get back to AOL, close the browser and click back to the previous AOL menu. Another problem to keep in mind: when you type a word into AOL's keyword search bar that's not a bona-fide AOL keyword, AOL will often toss you out onto the Internet. Very often it will toss you onto somebody's retail Web site. That's what happens if you type *needlecrafts* into the search bar, for example.

Viewing Quilting Web Pages Through AOL

To visit the quilting Web pages of AOL quilters head to Hometown AOL (**http://hometown.aol.com**). Search for "quilting."

HOW TO TAP INTO QUILTING FORUMS ON AMERICA ONLINE

*Note: On AOL you can use keywords to speed you to forums and special areas on the service. Type the keywords in the keyword box at the top of your AOL screen, or press **Ctrl-K** or ⌘-K on a Mac.*

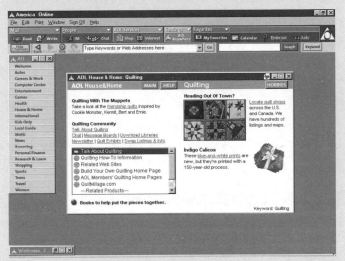

*Use the keyword **quilting** to get to the main menu of the quilting forum on AOL. That's where you'll find free patterns, advice, and even chat rooms for quilters to hang out.*

Head to the quilters' message boards in the quilting forum to chat with other quilters.

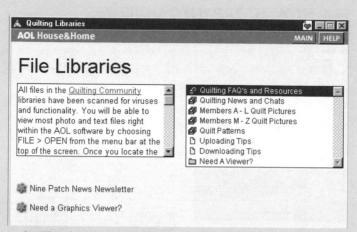

In the **File Libraries** of the quilting forum, you'll find free patterns as well as quilting advice to download. You can also download any necessary graphic viewers to view and print quilt patterns.

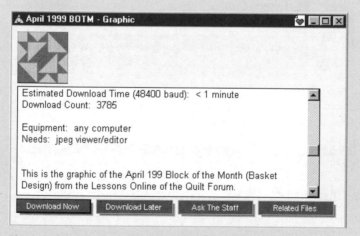

The AOL quilting forum hosts block-of-the-month exchanges and you can download past and present blocks in the file library.

Use the keyword **crafts** to get to the main menu of the general crafts forum. You'll find craft projects, plus links to other special crafts areas, such as scrapbooking.

Use the keyword **sewing** to get to the main needlecrafts menu on AOL. You'll find discussions, projects, and pattern libraries for many different sorts of needlecrafts, including knitting, crocheting, and cross-stitching.

Other keywords that will get you to quilting and craft forums on AOL:

Keyword: CraftBiz
Visit Janet Attard's Business Know-How forum to join discussions about running a craft business.

Keyword: WD or womans day
Woman's Day magazine offers a message board and occasional free quilting patterns and instructions.

Create shortcuts to your favorite quilting spots on AOL.

You can create toolbar buttons that will take you to your favorite forums on AOL with one click. When the

quilting forum main menu is displayed, rest your mouse cursor on the heart in the upper right hand corner.

Holding down the mouse button, drag the heart to your AOL toolbar at the top of the screen.

AOL will ask you to choose an icon for your new button and to label it. Once that's done, to get to the quilting forum simply click on it.

HOW TO GET TO QUILTING INFORMATION ON THE INTERNET FROM AOL

To get out onto the Internet from AOL, merely type the keyword *internet* in the keyword box at the top of the screen. That will pop up a menu in which you can type a Web page address, or head to other Internet attractions like Usenet discussion groups.

The AOL keyword box is very simply the first white box in the AOL toolbar into which one can type something. You can type AOL keywords there to whiz you to forums on the service—or Web page addresses to take you to pages on the World Wide Web.

TO GET TO QUILTING WEB PAGES...

A simpler way is to just type a Web page address into the keyword box at the top of the AOL screen. That will pop up AOL's Web browser. To get to other Web pages, type the address into the keyword box.

You can bookmark a Web page by dragging the heart in the upper right hand corner of AOL's browser window and dropping it onto the AOL toolbar, just as you can create shortcuts to forums.

The browser that's built into America Online's software is clunky, but you can use Netscape instead. Once you're connected to AOL, minimize the AOL software and fire up Netscape instead.

TO READ THE USENET NEEDLECRAFTS DISCUSSION GROUPS...

Type *usenet* into the AOL keyword box, then follow our directions in Chapter 3, page 63, for searching and subscribing to needlecraft newsgroups.

MORE TIPS FOR VIEWING QUILTING WEB PAGES THROUGH AOL

Sometimes when you visit Web pages outside of AOL, their pictures may look smeary or may not appear at all. Here are tips for troubleshooting AOL picture problems on the Web:

Clear Up Smeary Pictures: If you use Internet Explorer 5 to surf the Web with AOL, you may have noticed that IE 5 sometimes has problems displaying Web graphics. The culprit is AOL's graphics compression. Turn it off by heading to My AOL/Preferences and clicking the WWW icon. Head to the Web Graphics tab and remove the check beside "Use compressed graphics." Click Apply.

Clean Out Your Cache: Clean out AOL's cache directories and files regularly to keep the software from slowing down on the Web. Click My AOL, select Preferences and click WWW. Under the General tab, click Delete Files under Temporary Internet Files, and under History click the Clear History button. While you're there click the Settings button under Temporary Internet Files and reduce the "amount of disk space to use" to store Web graphics to about 50 megabytes. A large cache file can slow down your Web sessions. Run Scandisk weekly.

Try a Different Browser: If you'd rather surf the Web with Microsoft's Internet Explorer or Netscape, once you connect to AOL minimize the AOL software and fire up your favorite browser instead.

Power Down to AOL 3.0: If AOL's software seems to run slowly on your PC and if you have an older computer—a 486 or an older Pentium—try installing an older version of AOL's software. You can download **AOL 3.0** from AOL's Web site (**http://www.aol.com**).

free Cyberspace Quilting Bees

Don't have time to join an old-fashioned quilting bee? Hop into cyberspace and join one of the dozens of quilting klatches that swirl through it. Many are just like the quilting clubs our mothers belonged to—members help each other with their stitching, but also share in each others' lives. It may seem improbable, but quilters form deep friendships through their computers. (Our friendship is an example.) More than penpals, quilters get together for quilting shows and shopping trips, they cheer each other on through life's challenges and victories. Some of us can't imagine what life would be like without our quilting cyber-pals. We think that if you're not online already you owe it to yourself to plug in your modem and join the fun.

Best of all, you can participate in these guilds in your bathrobe and slippers—and you don't need to bring a dessert.

Note: Throughout this book we've used the quilting bee icon to note Web sites that offer chatting features, E-mail lists, or bulletin boards for quilters.

There are four different ways you can communicate with other quilters in cyberspace:

Web Site Bulletin Boards—You tap into a quilting Web site and read and reply to messages that are posted on the Web site.

Mailing Lists—Think of a mailing list as lots of E-mail messages copied to lots of people. Once you sign up for a list, the discussions come to your E-mail box. Mailing lists are normally where the best information is shared on the Internet on just about any topic, but especially in quilting.

Chat Rooms and the Like—Some quilt Web sites host guests that you can chat with computer CB-style. You'll also find active quilting chat rooms on America Online, and you can read about them in Chapter 2. We've also included directions on how to get started using ICQ, the most popular form of Internet relay chat.

Usenet Newsgroups—These are discussion groups that swirl through the Internet in a fairly anarchic fashion. There are tens of thousands of such discussion groups on various topics. There's a newsgroup devoted to quilting, and several others that discuss other needlework topics. But in general, quilters prefer mailing lists and chat rooms over newsgroups. You tap in by setting up your Web browser to download the messages from your Internet service. Or, if you use America Online, you can follow the AOL menus to the Usenet discussions. You'll find step-by-step instructions later in this chapter. You can also read newsgroups by tapping in through certain Web sites, and we tell you how to find those later in this chapter.

Web Message Boards Where You Can Chat With Other Quilters

Some of the big Web sites for quilters host message boards where you can write and reply to messages penned by quilters around the globe. Delphi's Quilting Arts Forum and the National Online Quilters are the two liveliest—they're essentially cyberspace quilt guilds. Some of these sites are quite marvelous, and offer many things besides good conversation, like patterns and information file libraries, regular feature articles and guests. Best of all, they're simple to tap into. Once you get to the Web addresses listed below, click the "forum" or "message board" button or link to find the conversations.

DELPHI'S QUILTING ARTS FORUM
http://www.delphi.com/quilting

Judy Smith hosts this electronic quilting guild extraordinaire. Blocks-of-the-month, message boards, fabric and block swaps, free patterns and more are the fare. You'll also find chats and a mailing list to join.

DELPHI'S SEWING FORUM
http://www.delphi.com/needle

Judy also hosts this mega-site where you'll find free patterns, projects, tips, and of course lots of wonderful conversation.

DELPHI'S TEXTILE ARTS FORUM
http://www.delphi.com/textile

Run by Rita Levine, this group discusses just about everything under the moon related to textiles. It has a wonderful library, and lots of wonderful people online.

NATIONAL ONLINE QUILTERS
http://www.noqers.org

This is an especially lively online quilt guild run by Cheryl Simmerman. You'll find projects, challenges, a library of files to download, like demos of quilting software, and an active message board.

THE ARTS & CRAFTS SOCIETY
http://www.arts-crafts.com

You'll find some very eclectic discussions on this Web site devoted to the Arts & Crafts movement—topics like block-printed fabrics and Frank Lloyd Wright-style textiles. Be sure to read the archives.

NANCY'S NOTIONS
http://www.nancysnotions.com

Tap into this Web site run by the Sewing with Nancy people for bulletin board-based discussions of fabric, sewing, quilting, and more.

SMALL EXPRESSIONS MESSAGE BOARD
http://www.small-expressions.com/bbs

David Small hosts this board where topics run from ladybug patterns to quilting frames.

BETTER HOMES & GARDENS DISCUSSIONS GROUPS
http://www.bhglive.com/talk.html

The American Patchwork and Quilting boards host discussions on friendly topics like "What quilt are you working on now?"

QUILTING AT ABOUT.COM MESSAGE BOARDS
http://quilting.about.com/hobbies/quilting/mpboards.htm

To join, complete a short, free membership form, then jump into reading and posting messages. Hosted by Susan Druding.

QUILTS BULLETIN BOARD
http://www.wwvisions.com/craftbb/quilts.html

QUILTING BOARD
FROM JO-ANN FABRICS AND CRAFTS
http://www.clothworld.com/share/fr_quilting.html

SCRAP QUILTS FORUM, HOSTED BY JANET WICKELL
http://www.delphi.com/scrappyquilts/start

T I P

Keep Your Browser and E-mail Programs Current to Keep Your Computer Secure Hardly a month goes by without someone finding a new security hole in a popular browser or E-mail program—and its maker quickly plugging it. Keep your software current by visiting the Web sites of their makers regularly and downloading any security patches or new versions. Be sure you download those only from their makers' Web sites. There have been reports of people receiving via E-mail "security patches" for Microsoft products that were actually hacker code to steal passwords. You can find out what version of Netscape you have by pulling down the Help menu and selecting About Communicator. If it's less than 4.5 you need to download a new version from **Netscape**'s Web site (**http://www.netscape.com**). If you're running Internet Explorer, from the Help menu select About Internet Explorer. If you're running a version prior to 5.0, you need to download a new copy from **Microsoft**'s Web site (**http://www.microsoft.com**).

How to Join the Quilting Mailing List Discussions

Special-interest mailing lists are where most knowledge is shared on the Internet. That's true for quilting, and for other subjects as well. We've sprinkled mailing list recommendations throughout this book. Here are some general-interest quilting mailing lists, and details of how to join them.

You should head to the Web page listed below to read the directions on how to join the list. In most instances you'll need to send an E-mail message to a computer that will add you to the mailing list. It will send you a confirmation message telling you that you're signed up. After that, any messages posted to the list will arrive in your mailbox each day.

KAFFEE-KLATSCH QUILT CHAT, HOSTED BY SUE TRAUDT
http://quilt.com/KaffeeKlatsch/KaffeeKlatsch.html

QUILTART, HOSTED BY JUDY SMITH
http://www.quiltart.com

Judy requests a $15 yearly contribution, but members of this list find it worth it to join.

QUILTERSBEE
http://www.quiltersbee.com/qbjoin.htm

THE SUNSHINE GUILD
http://sunshineguild.hypermart.net

QUILTCHAT LISTSERV
http://www.quiltchat.com/chat/maillist.html

QUILTNET
http://www.quilt.net

QUILTOPIA, HOSTED BY ROB HOLLAND
http://planetpatchwork.com/quiltop.htm

QUILTROPOLIS MAILING LISTS
http://www.quiltropolis.net/maillists/maillists.asp

Quiltropolis hosts over 40 mailing lists, many specifically for quilters, including: Crazy Quilt; WaterColor Quilting; Quilting 101; Appliqué; and Long Arm Quilting.

QUILT HERITAGE (TO DISCUSS QUILT HISTORY)
http://www.quilthistory.com

ELECTRIC QUILT
(TO DISCUSS THE USE OF EQ QUILT SOFTWARE)
http://www.wcnet.org/ElectricQuiltCo/Infoeq.htm
http://planetpatchwork.com/info-eq.htm

SEWPROS NETWORK FOR SEWING
ENTREPRENEURS, HOSTED BY KAREN MASLOWSKI
http://sewstorm.com/sewpros.htm

SCRAP QUILTS, HOSTED BY JANET WICKELL
http://www.UserHome.com/quilting/lilstitch.html

QUILTING FOR BEGINNERS, HOSTED BY SHIRLEY SOSTRE
http://www.sostre.com/beginnersquilts4.htm

THE FOUNDATION PIECER, HOSTED BY ZIPPY DESIGNS
https://www.zippydesigns.com/Forms/SubForm.html

QUILTSWAPPERS
http://www.quiltsville.com

KAYE WOOD MAILING LIST
http://www.kayewood.com/newsletter.html

QUILTER'S DREAM MAILING LIST
http://www.quiltersdream.com/MailingList.asp

FELTMAKERS LIST FAQ
http://www.peak.org/~spark/feltlistFAQ.html

InterQuilt Offers Quilting Fun, Camaraderie
Melissa Bishop's for-pay quilting cyber-bee **InterQuilt** (**http://kbs.net/tt/interquilt.html**) is a great list to join if you enjoy charity projects, swapping recipes with other quilters, and general quilting fun. Join for a free three-month trial. There is a small fee to continue your membership, but many quilters consider it worth it.

Find More Mailing Lists
To search for mailing list discussions in other interests head to **The Liszt** (**http://www.liszt.com**) or The List of Publicly Accessible Mailing Lists (**http://www.neosoft.com/internet/paml**).

🐝 QUILTING MAILING LISTS ARE FUN, INFORMATIVE, BUT YOU NEED TO FOLLOW THE RULES

No matter what your interests, mailing lists are your best source of information on the Internet. But before you sign up for one, you should read its rules for joining and posting to the list. Then follow our tips on mailing list netiquette.

• **When you join a mailing list, the computer that runs the list will automatically mail you directions for participating. Print them, and keep them near at hand.** Take note of the list's different E-mail addresses. You will be sending mail to one address, and sending any subscription changes to a different "administrative" address. *Don't send messages to subscribe or unsubscribe to the list to the address that will broadcast your message to everyone on the list!*

• **You probably have only a limited amount of disk space on your Internet service to store incoming E-mail. That means that if you're a member of a mailing list that generates lots of mail, the mail may overrun your mailbox if you don't check your E-mail daily.** When that happens, E-mail that people send you will bounce back to them. And the list may automatically unsubscribe you because messages are bouncing back. The solution: subscribe to the digest version of the list, if one is available, and unsubscribe from the list if you're going out of town.

• **Don't use free E-mail services like Juno or Hotmail to join mailing lists.** These services permit you to receive only a limited amount of E-mail, and when the list mail starts to overrun your mailbox the mailing list is going to bump you off the list. In fact, some mailing list owners will not permit subscribers with E-mail address on services like Yahoo! or Hotmail.

- **If the mailing list has rules about how mail to the list should be addressed, follow them.** Many lists request that members include the list's name in the Subject: line of any messages so that members who have set up their E-mail software to filter messages can do so effectively. You should also try to make the Subject: line of your message as informative as possible for readers who don't have time to read every message posted to the list.

- **Never include your address, phone number or other personal information in a mailing list post.** Many mailing lists are archived—which means that everyone on the Internet might be able to read them until the end of time!

- **When replying to a message, before you hit the Send button take a look at the message's address to check where it's going.** Don't send a personal reply to everyone on the mailing list. And don't hit Reply to All if the message is addressed to many different people or lists.

- **Never forward to the mailing list warnings of computer viruses, requests for charitable donations, or other chain letters.** Most chain letters, even those reporting computer viruses, are a hoax. (You can read more about these hoaxes at the **Urban Legends Archive** at **http://www.urbanlegends.com**.) If you feel compelled to forward a virus warning to your mailing list friends, send it first as a personal message to the list owner and ask her to forward it to the rest of the list if appropriate. The same rule applies to requests for charitable donations. Forward them first to the list owner and ask her to consider posting it to the list.

Here are a few mailing list terms you might encounter:

Moderated List—All messages that are mailed to the list are first sent to a moderator to screen before being broadcast to everyone on the list. No, it's not censorship, but merely a tactic to keep messages to the topic under discussion, and on some lists to prevent "flame wars" from breaking out between disagreeing members.

Unmoderated List—Messages are not screened.

Digest—Messages are collected into one long E-mail message that is sent at the end of the day to members who subscribe to the list's "digest version."

Archive—Some mailing list messages are stored in vast libraries on a Web site for others to search and read years later.

FAQ—Most lists have a "frequently asked question" file that contains questions to answers that list members commonly ask. Usually the FAQ is stored on the list's Web site, although some lists allow members to retrieve the file through E-mail.

Head to Free Sewing Machine Help, Chapter 21 for more E-mail mailing lists devoted to the love and care of sewing machines.

You're Never Too Old for a Secret Pal
Several of the quilting mailing lists and Web-based guilds conduct "angel" programs. Quilters are assigned secret pals who remember their birthdays, send them fat quarters and other gifties, and, at the extreme, are directed to "look out" for their charge on the Internet. Who told you there is no such thing as a fairy godmother?

How to Jump Into the Conversations in Quilting Chat Rooms

Chat, or "Internet relay chat," is what happens when two or more people carry on a conversation by typing to each other while logged into the Internet. There are several Web sites devoted to conducting quilting chats. Chats often occur on specific days and scheduled times, and may include guests such as quilt teachers or artists.

In order to participate you may need to download special chat software, or run up-to-date versions of Netscape or Internet Explorer and have Java enabled. The chat's official Web site will fill you in on what you need to do. The sites often have directions on how to join the conversation if you're connecting to the Web via TV. Log into these Web sites for more information and chat schedules.

QUILTCHAT BY KATHY SOMERS
http://www.quiltchat.com

AUNTIE'S QUILT CHAT
http://www.auntie.com/quiltchat.htm

QUILTTALK, SPONSORED BY QUILT MAGAZINE
http://www.quilttalk.com

QUILTROPOLIS CHAT
http://www.quiltropolis.com

NATIONAL ONLINE QUILTERS CHAT
http://www.noqers.org/talkcity.html

ABOUT.COM QUILTING CHAT
http://quilting.about.com/mpchat.htm

🛒 FABRIC STASH
http://fabric-stash.com

DELPHI'S QUILTING CHAT
http://www.delphi.com/quilting

DELPHI'S TEXTILE ARTS CHAT
http://www.delphi.com/textile

DELPHI'S SEWING CHAT
http://www.delphi.com/needle

QUILTING AND SEWING
WITH KAYE WOOD WEEKLY CHAT
http://www.kayewood.com

T I P

Help Finding Lost Quilts

If you're looking for a recently lost quilt, or know of a homeless one that has been found, head to **The Lost Quilt Come Home Page** (**http://www.lostquilt.com**) or Quilt Lost & Found (**http://www2.succeed.net/~amc/quilts.html**).

Netscape: Free Quilt Chat Room – Quilters Chat

Location: http://quilting.about.com/hobbies/quilting/mpchat.htm   What's Related

About.
The Human Internet™

You are here: About > Hobbies > Quilting

Quilting
with Susan C. Druding Your Guide to One of Over 700 Sites

Search for [_____] in this topic site [Go]

Home · Recent Articles · Visit Forums · Chat Live · Contact Guide · Free Newsletter

Subjects
Applique
Beginners
Books Magazines
Charity Quilting
Classes Workshops
ClipArt Graphics
Collecting & Care
Fabrics Online
Competitions
Computers-Software
Quilting Community
Doll making
Dyeing - All Types
Foundation Piecing
Free Blocks
Free Small Quilts
Free Projects
Internat'l Quilt
Quilt Equipment
Holiday
Fun Humor
Quilts Galleries
GuildsAssociations
Young Quilters

Log on to Chat

How to Chat | F.A.Q. | User Agreement | Guidelines | Chat Support

Can't see the entire chat window in your monitor? Just Click the Float button.

Welcome to Our Free Quilt Chat Room for Quilting at About.com

The Chat room is open everyday. You are welcome to use the chat area to meet friends on your own as well as to attend scheduled chats. You will need to have a Java-based browser.

Pfaffers Chat here every Monday evening - 10:00 pm Eastern Std Time, 7 pm Pacific Time
Quilters Chat here every Wednesday evening - 9:15 Eastern Std Time, 6:15 Pacific Time
Plus there are quilters in the Chat room many other evenings as well, so drop in, see who is here and get acquainted.

If you are from outside the USA we are trying to get an International time period set up for Europe and South Pacific - so come to the free Quilting Discussion Forum and leave a message of your interest to chat in other time periods.

Related Sites
from About & Partners
Antiques
Arts/Crafts Business
Basketry
Beadwork
Decorative Arts
Folk Art
Interior Decorating
Knitting
Needlepoint
Sewing

Also Recommended
Apply to become a partner for this site.

Magazine Offer

About.Com's Quilting Forum (**http://quilting.about.com**) hosts online chats every week. To participate you need only to be running version 3.x or higher of Netscape or Internet Explorer, and you must have Java enabled. Other sewing sites also offer chat rooms. To participate you may need to download special software. You'll need to read the directions on the Web site to find out how to join in.

Some Quilters Keep in Touch with ICQ

ICQ, named after "I Seek You," is a free chat program similar to America Online's Instant Messenger. Once you install it, whenever you tap into the Internet, it "logs" you into the ICQ network, informing your friends that you've come online—and informing you if they're online. Many quilters use it to keep in touch. In fact, you may spot ICQ "call numbers" at the end of quilters' E-mail messages. With ICQ, you can send each other instant messages, exchange files, and chat as if you were both in an Internet chat room. It offers a number of privacy features that go beyond those in AOL's Instant Messenger. You can set ICQ to tell friends that you're online, but don't wish to be disturbed, for instance. You can also set ICQ to prevent strangers from sending you unsolicited messages. You can download ICQ in both PC and Mac flavors from **ICQ.com** (**http://web.icq.com**). You can also tap into quilting discussions and find other quilters through the ICQ Web site. Use the search box to search for "quilting."

How to Join Usenet Quilting Discussions

Newsgroups are public discussion groups that you read with your Web browser's news reader. In general, quilting and sewing newsgroups are less personable and chatty in tone than mailing lists. (We think they're less fun.) But quilters share valuable information in them nevertheless. Here's a list of newsgroups of interest to quilters:

rec.crafts.textiles.quilting
Anything having to do with quilting

rec.crafts.textiles.needlework
Any form of hand-stitching is discussed

rec.crafts.textiles.sewing
Sewing clothes, furnishings, etc.

rec.crafts.textiles.yarn
Any craft involved with yarn

rec.crafts.textiles.misc
Miscellaneous fiber and textile discussions

rec.crafts.marketplace
Small ads for craft products

uk.rec.crafts
Hobnob with United Kingdom crafters

How to Read Usenet Quilting Newsgroups with Your Web Browser

Tapping into the Usenet newsgroups can be tricky. You need to set up your browser to download the groups from your Internet service, then use your browser's mail reader to read them.

The first time you want to read a newsgroup you'll need to download from your ISP a complete list of current newsgroups. Then you'll need to search it and subscribe to the groups you're interested in. Finally, you need to download the messages themselves. Here's how to do it with Netscape and Explorer:

How to Read the Needlecraft Newsgroups with Netscape

1. You must first set up your browser to retrieve newsgroups from your Internet server. Find out from your Internet server the name of the computer where newgroups are stored. (It will be something like **groups.myisp.com**.) Pull down the **Edit** menu and select **Preferences**. Under **Mail & Newsgroups**, head to the **Newsgroup Servers** or **Group Server** setup box and click **Add**. Type the name of your ISP's newsgroup server. Click **OK** to save it.

2. Connect to your Internet service.

3. Head to Navigator's message center by pressing **Ctrl-2** or click the **Mail** icon box in the lower-right corner of the browser screen on a Mac.

4. From the **File** menu, select **Subscribe to Discussion Groups**.

5. Click the **All** or **All Groups** tab to download a list of current newsgroups. This may take a while since the list is large. The message "Receiving discussion groups" should appear on the very bottom line of the screen. Hit the **Refresh List** button if you or someone else in your household has set up the news-reader to subscribe to mailing lists in the past.

6. When that humongous list of newsgroups has finished downloading, head to the **Search for a Group** tab. Type a word to search for, such as "quilting"—or type "rec.crafts.tex-tiles" for a list of all the needlework newsgroups. Click the **Search Now** button.

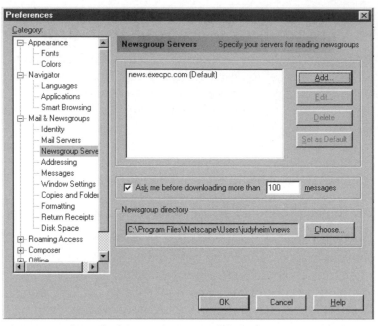

First you need to tell Navigator the name of the server on your ISP where newsgroups are stored.

7. Once the newsgroup searcher has come up with a list of interesting newsgroups, highlight the one you want to read, and press the **Subscribe** button. A check will appear beside it.

8. To read your newsgroup, head back to the message center (**ctrl-2** or click the **Mail** icon box on a Mac). From the pull-down menu box at the top of the screen, select the newsgroup and click **Download Messages**. Or click the **Get Msg** icon. You may want to download only a selection (under 500 for example) and mark as read the rest of the messages. This way, the next time you download messages from the newsgroup, you will only download the newest ones.

9. From the **Go** menu you can move from thread to thread, reading messages and skipping others.

10. In the future to read messages, go to the message center (**ctrl-2** or click the **Mail** icon box on a Mac). From the pull-down menu box at the top of the screen, select the newsgroup you want to read. From the **File** menu select **Get Messages/Now**.

You need to download the complete list of newsgroups in order to search for the ones you're interested in.

Search for the newsgroup list by heading to the search tab. After you've located newsgroups you'd like to read, subscribe to them by selecting them. You can click through the list just as you'd click through subdirectories on your computer.

Select the messages and message threads you want to read and they'll appear in the bottom of the screen. (If you don't get a split screen you may need to "pull up" the bottom portion of the screen with your mouse. In other words, the window is there, it's just hidden.)

Here's a Simple Way to Read Needlework Newsgroups You can read newsgroups from the comfort of your Web browser by heading to Google.Com (**http://groups.google.com**) or Deja.Com (**http://www.deja.com/usenet**). Reading them through these Web sites isn't as easy as reading them with your browser's newsreader, but it is a simple way to access the groups. Search for the newsgroup's name, such as rec.crafts.textiles.quilting. Or, search for words like "quilting" or "sewing." In addition to current newsgroup messages, you'll find an archive of past messages going back to just about the beginning of time and which you can search for past conversations and advice.

How to Read the Needlecraft Newsgroups with Microsoft Explorer

1. Load the Outlook Express mail portion of Internet Explorer by clicking on the mailbox icon on the top right-hand corner of the screen. Click the **Read News** icon on the Express screen. If you have not yet set it up to

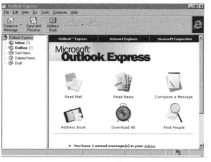

read newsgroups with your ISP, a setup wizard will appear. It will prompt you for your name, E-mail address, and the name of the dial-up connection you use to connect to your ISP. Most important of all it will ask you the name of the server on your ISP where the news messages can be found.

2. The next time you click **Express's Read News** icon it will ask you if you'd like to download a list of the newsgroups from your ISP. This may take a while since there are tens of thousands of newsgroups.

> ✋ **Warning!** If you try to download more than about 500 newsgroup messages with Explorer it will crash.

T I P

Looking for More Sewing Resources on the Web? Visit **Sew City** (**http://www.sewcity.com**) where you'll find a directory of links to Web sites related to fabric, patterns, interior design, and more.

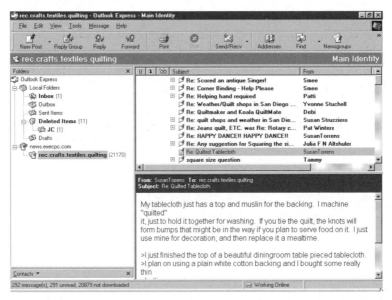

3. Type "rec.crafts.textiles" or some other word to search for, or type names of newsgroups from the table. Subscribe to them by highlighting each, clicking the **Subscribe** button. Then click **OK** when you're done.

4. To read newsgroups that you've subscribed to, click the **Go To** button. Or, click on the name of the newsgroup on the left side of the screen. To read individual messages, click on the headers displayed at the top right of the screen.

How to Read the Needlecraft Newsgroups on America Online

1. To read the Internet newsgroups through AOL press **ctrl-k** or **⌘-K** on a Mac and type the keyword newsgroups. Or, type it in the keyword box at the top of the

screen. Click the **Search All Newsgroups** icon to search the tens of thousands of newsgroups for ones in your interests.

2. Type "rec.crafts.textiles" and AOL will display all the needlework newsgroups. Click the name of the news-group and click "Subscribe to news-group." Depending

upon which version of AOL's software you're using you can read the messages in the newly subscribed newsgroup imme-diately, or else you'll need to head back to the main news-group menu by closing the windows (click the **X** in the upper right-hand corner). Click the **Read My Newsgroups** button to pop up a list of the newsgroups to which you're sub-scribed. Click the **List Unread** button to list messages in the newsgroups that you have not yet read.

3. To read listed mes-sages click the title of the message.

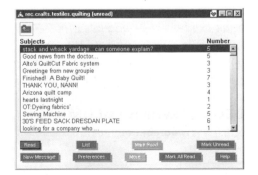

freeBig Quilting Web Sites

If you're just getting started on the Web where should you go first? The quilting Web sites in this chapter, we think. They have everything: free patterns, lots of tips, monthly block and fabric swaps, good conversations, and lots of friendly quilters. In the beginning of this book we warn that Web sites come and go and it is unavoidable that some of the addresses in this book are bound to be gone by the time you look for them. The Web sites in this chapter have been around so long they're institutions. Bookmark them in your browser, and know that they'll be there when you need them.

All these sites also offer hotlinks to all the newest and neatest quilting stuff on the Internet. Consider them portals into the quilting world in cyberspace. While you're visiting be sure to drop a note of gratitude to the site's "webmistress" or master. The quilters who run these mega-sites do so for little or no compensation—and running sites like this can be a full-time job.

DELPHI TEXTILE ARTS FORUM
http://www.delphi.com/textile

One of the first commercial online services ever was a quirky (but cheap) service known as Delphi. It attracted a carefree, if intense group of quilters, sewers, spinners, and knitters. Delphi's conversational forums are now available for free through the Web. They've blossomed into incredible resources with files, conversations, magazine-like features—and lots of knowledgeable people everywhere. The quilting and sewing forums are run by Judy Smith, the textile one by Rita Levine. You can tap in through their Web pages, and they're all worth checking out.

DELPHI SEWING FORUM
http://www.delphi.com/needle

SUE TRAUDT'S WORLD WIDE QUILTING PAGE
http://quilt.com/MainQuiltingPage.html

Sue's was the first quilting page on the Web, and it continues to be the best. Sue has everything on her site: frequently-asked question files from quilting mailing lists; links to just about everything the Internet offers quilters; plus lots and lots of free patterns and advice.

QUILTCHAT
http://kathkwilts.com

Quiltchat is an Internet "chat" channel for quilters, but you don't need to participate in chats to find friends and information at this huge Web site for quilters, run by Kathy Somers.

GET CREATIVE

This huge sewing and quilting site offers articles, project sheets, and free patterns.

NATIONAL ONLINE QUILTERS
http://www.noqers.org

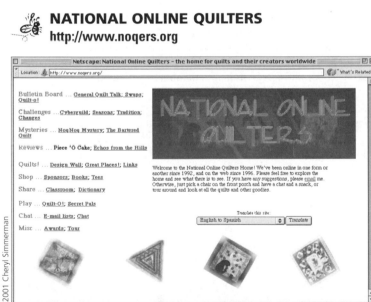

© 2001 Cheryl Simmerman

Cheryl Simmerman runs this beehive of quilters who've been together for years. You'll love the chatter, and the swaps. The news and features are as good as in any quilting magazine.

QUILTING AT ABOUT.COM
http://quilting.about.com

Susan Druding of San Francisco's Straw Into Gold is the quilting "guide" at this pre-eminent leisure-interest Web site. You'll find Susan's weekly articles, plus links, patterns, tips, and much, much more. There's even a bulletin board and chat feature. While you're at About.Com check out its other special interest pages like *Sewing* (**http://sewing.about.com**) and *Arts & Crafts Business* (**http://artsandcrafts.about.com**). To find portions of this sometimes-hard-to-navigate Web site devoted to your other needlecraft interests head to its hobby index page (**http://home.about.com/hobbies**).

QUILTER'S ONLINE RESOURCE
http://www.nmia.com/~mgdesign/qor/index.html

Mary Graham runs this Web site which is full of patterns, projects, news, tips, and chatter.

QUILTERSBEE
http://www.quiltersbee.com

The QuiltersBee Web site is devoted to the mailing list of the same name. Among the activities of this 800+ member quilting sorority: a birthday club, "secret angels," mystery quilts, and fabric and block swaps galore. The site offers a nice directory of links to other quilting sites on the Web.

DELPHI QUILTING FORUM
http://www.delphi.com/quilting

> **Looking for a Fabric by Your Favorite Designer?**
> Many fabric designers offer on their Web sites features that let you track down local stores that carry their fabrics. Some also offer features that will track down discontinued fabrics and fabric lines for you. An example is the Fabric Finder feature on **Jinny Beyer's Web site** (**http://www.jinnybeyer.com/fabric/fabricfinder.cfm**). If you don't know the URL for the Web site of the designer, try entering the designer's name in a search engine like **Google** (**http://www.google.com**).

> **Racing Around Looking for Fabric to Finish a Quilt?**
> You know the sick feeling: You need just a quarter yard of a particular print to finish piecing a quilt, but your quilt store no longer carries it. Head to Pat Knox's **Missing Fabric Page** (**http://www.missingfabric.com**) to locate other quilters who may have that little piece you need.

QUILTART
http://www.quiltart.com

QuiltArt is a popular mailing list-based discussion group for quilters who like to stretch the bounds of tradition. Head to Chapter 3 for directions on how to tap into a mailing list. You'll find on the list's Web site news and resources for quilters of all persuasions.

PLANET PATCHWORK
http://www.planetpatchwork.com

Rob Holland's Planet is the home to his E-zine Virtual Quilter. But Rob offers lots of other good stuff, including links to all the good quilting stuff on the Web.

WEB SITES OF FAVORITE QUILTING & SEWING TV SHOWS

Many of the popular TV quilting and craft shows host Web sites where you can find archives of free patterns and directions for projects that have been featured on past shows. Some also include information on products used in the show, with hotlinks to the manufacturer's Web sites.

AMERICA QUILTS
http://www.pbs.org/americaquilts

ELEANOR BURNS' QUILT-IN-A-DAY
http://www.quilt-in-a-day.com/tv

HOME & GARDEN NETWORK
http://www.hgtv.com

HGTV hosts a nearly 24-hour roster of home-related cable TV shows, and its Web site is a goldmine of special features and schedules for the shows. You'll find special pages devoted to each of its shows, many including project instructions, how-to information, and even chats. Some popular shows quilters will enjoy include:

- **SIMPLY QUILTS, WITH ALEX ANDERSON**
- **THE CAROL DUVALL SHOW**
- **SEW PERFECT, WITH SANDRA BETZINA**

QUILTING FOR THE '90S, WITH KAYE WOOD
http://www.kayewood.com

QUILTING FROM THE HEARTLAND
http://www.qheartland.com/project.htm

BETTER HOMES & GARDENS TELEVISION SHOW
http://www.bhglive.com/tv/index.html

SEWING WITH NANCY, WITH NANCY ZIEMAN
http://www.nancysnotions.com

SEW CREATIVE, WITH DONNA WILDER
http://www.poly-fil.com/sewcreative/SC.html

MARTHA'S SEWING ROOM
http://www.cptr.ua.edu/msr

MARTHA STEWART
http://www.marthastewart.com

how to Find More Great Web Sites of Quilters

Thousands of quilters display their handiwork on their Web sites. They also offer quilting advice, tips and free patterns. We couldn't include URLs for them all in this book (although we would have liked to). In this chapter you'll find some of our favorites, plus advice and links for tapping into the Web sites of quilters around the world.

To find other quilters on the Web, start by tapping into the big quilting Web sites we recommend in the previous chapter. Many of these sites contain directories to the quilt sites of individual quilters.

Then take a look at the Web sites for the big quilting discussion groups—you'll find them in Chapter 3 on cyberspace quilting bees. Most of these sites also include directories of members' Web sites.

Find Web Pages of Quilters on America Online Hundreds of quilters host Web pages through America Online. You'll find on their pages free patterns and quilting advice, as well as links to other quilting info on the Web. To find them, if you're on AOL use the keywords "hometown aol." If you're not on AOL head to: **http://hometown.aol.com**.

Surf Quilting Web Rings to Visit the Web Pages of Quilters A Web ring is a collection of Web pages of enthusiasts who have decided to link together. There are a number of Web rings for quilters, including one for Web pages devoted to quilting swaps and a ring of Web pages with information on long-armed quilting. To find them head to **Yahoo! WebRing** (**http://dir.webring.yahoo.com**). Use the search box near the bottom of the page to search for "quilts" or "quilting." You don't have to "join" a ring (or Yahoo!) to surf its Web pages. Just click the ring's icon and you're off. Here are more quilters' Web rings:

QUILT PATTERN DESIGNERS COLLECTIVE
http://www.quiltseeds.com/designers%20webring.htm

QUILT A ROUND WEB RING
http://members.tripod.com/~TigerRose/joinring.html

QUILTWOMAN.COM
http://www.quiltwoman.com

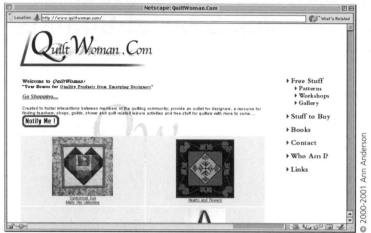

Ann Anderson, who really wanted to be Wonder Woman, runs a delightful site that includes free patterns, tips, workshops, and a bulletin board.

QUILTAHOLICS
http://www.quiltaholics.com

Deb Kauffunger's Quiltaholics site offers projects, lessons, tips, and "confessions of a quiltaholic."

SCRAP QUILTS

Janet Wickell maintains this marvelous resource for lovers of scrap quilts. It includes free patterns, instruction, a forum, swaps, and more.

QUILTS LIMITED
http://www.quiltslimited.com

You'll find an extensive collection of tips and instruction, plenty of courses, a free mailing list to join, and more.

FCREATE QUILT
http://member.nifty.ne.jp/GUCKY/e_index.html

Visit Japanese quilters at this Web incarnation of the quilters club on the large Japanese online service NIFTY-Serve.

QUILT ETHNIC.COM
http://www.quiltethnic.com

A guide to the fascinating and diverse quilting and related fiber arts of various ethnic groups, including African, Haitian, African-American, Latin American, Asian, and Native American.

QUILTER'S VILLAGE
http://www.quiltersvillage.com

Quilter's Village is a gateway to favorite publications such as Quilter's Newsletter Magazine and McCall's Quilting. You'll find some terrific free projects, plus quilting tips and other resources.

QUILT MAGIC
http://ecuador.junglevision.com/carolyn/qhp.htm

Carolyn Hill celebrates the magic of quiltmaking at her inspiring site where you can read stories about quilting and view quilts. Tap in and share your quilting story.

JINNY BEYER STUDIO
http://www.jinnybeyer.com

Jinny shares free patterns, tips, instructions, and offers information on her fabrics, seminar, books and videos.

THE QUILT CHANNEL
http://www.quiltchannel.com

This joint project of Quiltropolis and Planet Patchwork offers a searchable collection of quilt-related Web sites.

T I P

You Know You're a Quilter When... You know you're a quilter when you buy chocolates in heart-shaped boxes that you can use as quilting templates. Read this "collected wisdom" from members of QuiltNet, courtesy of **Sue Traudt's World Wide Quilting** (**http://ttsw.com/MiscQuilting/YouKnow.html**).

ALEX ANDERSON QUILTS
http://www.alexandersonquilts.com

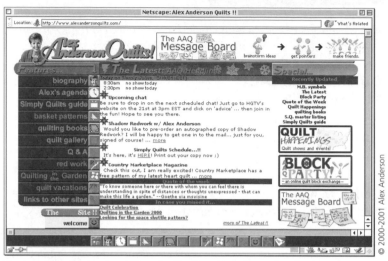

Host of the popular show **Simply Quilts,** *Alex shares free basket patterns and news of quilt happenings, and offers an online block exchange.*

QUILTING FOR BEGINNERS BY BEGINNERS
http://www.sostre.com/beginnersquilts.htm

Shirley Sostre runs this Web site for newbie quilters. She offers tips, techniques, swaps, and more.

QUILTS AND QUILTING, SUITE 101
http://www.suite101.com/welcome.cfm/quilts_and_quilting

Jeanne Walsh is your guide to quilting at this site that offers articles on quilting, a discussion forum, and links to Web sites of quilters.

THE CATS WHO QUILT WEB SITE
http://www.catswhoquilt.com

Judy's Web site offers links to free cat quilt patterns that can be found around the Web, fabric stores where you can buy cat-themed fabrics, and cat quilt "doings" around cyberspace.

SUSAN DRUDING'S QUILTING AND PFAFF, AND FIBER PAGE
http://members.tripod.com/~druding

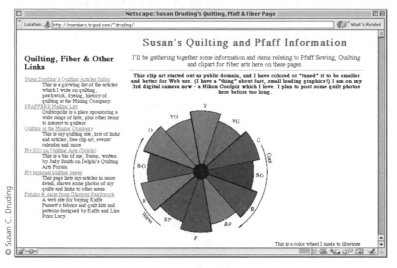

Read Susan's quilting articles, browse items related to quilting with a Pfaff, download quilting clipart and tap into the linked Web sites of other quilters.

QUILTING DIRECTORY
http://www.quiltingdirectory.co.uk

The United Kingdom's premier quilting resource on the Web where you'll find links to UK quilt shops, message boards, and articles.

free Quilting Patterns

What quilter doesn't want every quilt pattern in the universe? Click your way around the Internet and you'll have them soon enough. Oodles of free quilt patterns, from traditional pieced to holiday appliqué float through cyberspace. Some are products of quilt magazines and publishers, others have been drawn by famous designers and ordinary quilters like you and me.

Just remember that if you print these patterns to give to friends, always include the name and Web site address of the designer, and any applicable copyright notices. Most of these patterns are provided for "personal use" only. If you want to hand them out free at a store or quilt guild meeting, always ask the owner for permission first. The owners of many of these Web sites change their patterns regularly, so be sure to drop in frequently.

And remember: whenever you print or save to disk a quilt pattern, always drop an E-mail of thanks to the Web site owner.

For help on displaying the patterns, enlarging them, and printing them, head to our tutorials in Chapter 1.

Note: Since pattern URLs change often, head to the root of the URL if the pattern URL spits out an error. For example, head to **www.quiltbus.com** if you can't find anything at **www.quiltbus.com/Quilt%20Blocks.htm**.

Web Sites with Big Collections of Quilt Block Patterns

FREE QUILT BLOCKS FROM QUILT BUS
http://www.quiltbus.com/Quilt%20Blocks.htm

This site is a gateway to over 600 free quilt blocks located around the Web. Some blocks include rotary cutting instructions, speed piecing tips, and suggested layouts.

FREE STUFF FROM PATCHES, ETC.
http://www.patches3.com/freestuff.htm

A beautiful selection of cross-stitch and redwork patterns, perfect for quilt blocks.

BLOCKS GALORE FROM QUILTERS CACHE
http://www.quilterscache.com/QuiltBlocksGalore.html

THE TWELVE DAYS OF CHRISTMAS
FROM QUILTERS CACHE
http://www.quilterscache.com/QuiltBlocksGalore10.html

SUE TRAUDT'S WIDE WORLD QUILTING PAGE
http://quilt.com

Sue maintains an extensive directory of free patterns.

SUNBONNET SUE
http://sunbonnetsue.com

Tap into this site for a wonderful selection of free patterns and more—all dedicated to Sunbonnet Sue and Overall Bill.

30 BEAUTIFUL BLOCKS—
A BIRTHDAY CELEBRATION, BY MARY AUSTIN
http://www.quiltersnewsletter.com/qnm/feature4.htm

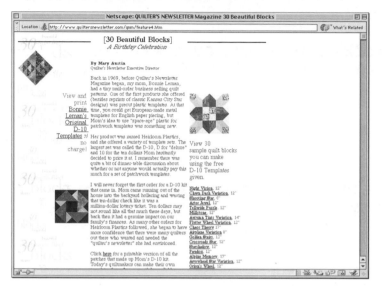

Here is a beautiful collection of blocks made using a specific set of templates.
You can view and print the original set of templates and view instructions for
the entire collection of blocks.

McCALL'S QUILTING BLOCKS
http://www.mccallsquilting.com/mccalls/bom/index.htm

CATS WHO QUILT FREE PATTERNS
http://www.execpc.com/~judyheim/free.html

Free cat-themed quilting patterns.

EK TUPPER'S QUILT BLOCK DIRECTIONS
http://users.tellurian.net/ektupper/patterns.htm

FREE PATTERNS FROM P&B TEXTILES
http://www.pbtex.com/html/free_patterns.html

ARTS AND QUILTS FREE QUILT PATTERN PAGE
http://www.artsandquilts.com/free_patterns.htm

PATTERNS FROM ALEX ANDERSON

http://www.alexandersonquilts.com
http://www.alexandersonquilts.com/blockparty/index.htm
http://www.alexandersonquilts.com/basket/basket.html

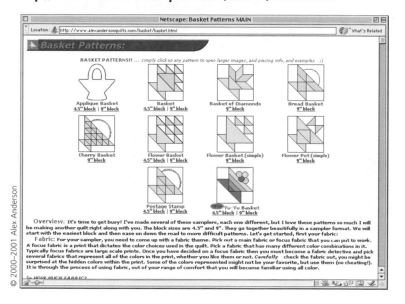

🛒 PICKLE DISH.COM

http://www.pickledish.com

Calling all Kansas City Star block fans, this site is for you.

FREE PATTERNS FROM PIECEFUL PLEASURES

http://www.piecefulpleasures.com/patterns.htm

FREE QUILTING PATTERNS FROM CRAFTOWN

http://www.craftown.com/quilt.htm

FREE PATTERNS FROM DUTCHMAN DESIGNS

http://www.dutdes.com/ddfree.html

SHINING STAR FROM QUILT IN A DAY

http://www.quilt-in-a-day.com/freepat

SCRAP QUILTS
http://www.scrapquilts.com

Janet Wickell offers complete instructions for several quilt projects, including scrappy baskets, a 9-patch variation, grandma's choice, 4-patch mock log cabins—and more.

FREE PATTERNS
FROM MARCUS BROTHERS TEXTILES, INC.
http://www.marcusbrothers.com/free_patterns/index.html

QUILT BLOCK COLLECTION
http://www.gotomywebpage.com/quiltdesigns/qbc.htm

QUILT BLOCKS FROM JOEN WOLFROM
http://www.mplx.com/joenwolfrom

CRAZY QUILTERS PATTERN PAGE
http://www.crazyquilters.com
http://www.crazyquilters.com/Patterns/patterns.html

PATCHPIECES PATTERNS AND PROJECTS
http://www.patchpieces.com/PPpatterns.html

Paper piecing and applique pattern libraries.

FREE PATTERNS FROM THE SUNSHINE QUILT GUILD
http://www.ssqa.org/fun.htm
http://sunshineguild.hypermart.net/patterns.htm

QUILT BLOCK PATTERNS
FROM HESTER BUTLER-EHLE
http://www.portup.com/~hjbe/quilt/qblox.html

BARBARA'S QUILT WORLD
http://home.online.no/~barbaras/quiltny.htm

LAURIE BENDER'S GOOD LIVING BLOCK LIBRARY
http://home.att.net/~LKBender/quilting.html

COMPUQUILT QUILT BLOCK CONSTRUCTION SITE
http://www.compuquilt.com/piecing.htm

PARTNERS IN PATCHWORK BIBLICAL BLOCKS
http://www.mountain-inter.net/~graham/partners.html

JINNY BEYER STUDIOS
http://www.jinnybeyer.com
http://www.jinnybeyer.com/free_patterns.cfm

Jinny Beyer offers a large selection of block and quilt patterns.

QUILTING PROJECTS FROM CRANSTON VILLAGE
http://www.cranstonvillage.com/quilt/projects/current/index.html
http://www.cranstonvillage.com

FREE PROJECTS FROM NANCY'S NOTIONS
http://www.nancysnotions.com

Nancy Zieman of Sewing With Nancy *fame offers free quilting and sewing patterns. Click the "free projects" link.*

DEBBIE MUMM'S PROJECT OF THE MONTH
http://www.debbiemumm.com/project_of_the_month/project_of_
  the_month.html

HOW TO TRACK DOWN HARD-TO-FIND QUILTING BOOKS ON THE WEB

One of the most common questions that we hear from quilters on the Web is "I'm looking for a quilting book by so-and-so. The publisher says it's out of print. How can I find it on the Web?" Here are some detective techniques to try:

Pay a visit to Bette S. Feinstein's Hard to Find Needlework Books (http://www.needleworkbooks.com). Bette is famous for her inventory of all sorts of impossible-to-find needlework books and magazines. If she doesn't have the book you're looking for in stock, drop her a note and she'll hunt it down for you.

Stop in at Bibliofind (http://www.bibliofind.com). You can find many out-of-print books through this amazing service, and they're reasonably priced too.

Search eBay (http://www.ebay.com). You'd be surprised at the selection of quilting books that pops up on this Web auction site. Be sure to check every week, for items on the service change quickly. Also read our tips in Chapter 1 for safe Web flea marketing.

Pay a visit to the Web site of Checker Distributors (http://www.checkerdistributors.com). Checker distributes craft books to stores, and they offer on their Web site a database of the books they carry—and links and information about the stores that carry specific titles.

Try these other Web sites that sell vintage needlework patterns:

BEKI'S SEWING PATTERNS
http://www.sewingpatterns.com

PATTERNS FROM THE PAST
http://www.oldpatterns.com

LILY ABELLO'S VINTAGE PATTERNS
http://www.lilyabello.com/patternshop

Post a note about the book to some of the quilting mailing lists we recommend in Chapter 3. Another quilter might have the book and be willing to sell it.

Still can't find the book? Try typing the name of the book or its author into a Web searcher like **Google** (**http://www.google.com**). You may be able to come up with a Web page for the author. Also do a search of the book-selling Web site **Amazon.Com** (**http://www.amazon.com**). Amazon's database lists just about every book in print. You might be able to come up with the name of other quilting books by the author. You can track down the author by contacting her current publisher. Sometimes authors have extra copies of a book they may want to sell, or they may have used in another book the pattern that you're looking for.

Take a Free Online Art Class

Visit **Wet Canvas** (**http://www.wetcanvas.com**) to take free courses in drawing, digital art, watercolors, design, and more (**http://www.wetcanvas.com/ArtSchool/index.html**). The site also offers over 200,000 links to art-related Web sites. Want to talk to others about art? Tap into the **Wet Canvas Forums** (**http://www.wetcanvas.com/cgi-bin/Ultimate.cgi**) where you'll find other artists discussing everything from *The Artist's Way* to art theory.

CONNECTING THREADS—
FREE PROJECT DOWNLOADS
http://www.connectingthreads.com
http://www.connectingthreads.com/ct/quilts/quilt_cat.asp

Click the Free Project Downloads link for an assortment of patterns including one for an Amish schoolhouse, a floral wreath, quilt pillows, and several other projects.

FREE PATTERNS.COM
http://www.freepatterns.com

You need to register to gain access to this collection—that means that you must type in your name and address. We didn't like that, especially since the site lacks a privacy policy. In other words, they don't tell you what they're going to do with your personal information. There are also lots of pop-up ads. But you can find some nice traditional quilting patterns here, such as one for a log cabin quilt. You need to have Adobe's Acrobat installed in order to view them.

PROJECTS FROM EZ QUILTING BY WRIGHTS
http://www.ezquilt.com

Select the projects link from the left menu for a collection of projects using a rotary cutter and specialized acrylic rulers.

QUILT PATTERNS FROM SOUTH SEA IMPORTS
http://www.southseaimports.com/projects.htm

There are a variety of quilting patterns from many well-known artists. You need Adobe Acrobat to view and print the patterns.

THE QUILTER MAGAZINE
FREE QUILT PATTERN ARCHIVE
http://www.thequiltermag.com/frproject.html

This magazine, formerly The Traditional Quilter, offers free patterns and directions for some lovely old-fashioned style quilts.

FREE PATTERNS FROM LUCY FAZELY
http://www.lucyfazely.com/free.html

FAIRFIELD PROJECTS
http://www.poly-fil.com/crafts/ProjectsAndInfo.html

You'll find a selection of home decor, craft and quilt projects from the makers of Poly-fil stuffing.

JO-ANN FABRICS' QUILTING PROJECT CENTER
http://www.fabricenters.com/project/quilting

You'll find a number of lovely quilting patterns here, including full instructions for assembly. You'll find patterns for several block-of-the-month series, including the Floralscape one which is an appliqué block.

NEW EXPRESSIVE QUILTING DESIGNS
FROM CENTRAL PRESS PUBLICATIONS
http://www.centralpress.com/free.html

A collection of free full-size downloadable quilting designs. You can use them for hand or machine quilting, or appliqué.

Web Sites with Free Patterns for Specific Types of Blocks

QUILTING PATTERNS FROM QUILTING MAGAZINE
http://www.quiltmag.com

- ## CATHEDRAL WINDOWS QUILT
BY DEBBY KRATOVIL
http://www.quiltmag.com/lessons/cathedral/cathedral_windows.html

- ## THREE-DIMENSIONAL BOW-TIES
BY DEBBY KRATOVIL
http://www.quiltmag.com/lessons/bowtie.html

- ## KALEIDOSCOPE BY DEBBY KRATOVIL
http://www.quiltmag.com/lessons/kaleidoscope/kaleidoscope.html

BROWN BAG QUILT BY SANDRA WHEELER
AND ANGEL THINGS DESIGNS
http://www.angelthings.com/brown_bag_quilt.htm

BUILDING A LOG CABIN
FROM VIRGINIA CONSORTIUM OF QUILTERS
http://www.vcq.org
http://www.vcq.org/specialty%20lessons.htm/log_cabin.htm

SUNBONNET SUE PROJECT OF THE MONTH
http://sunbonnetsue.com/monproject.html

CHRISTMAS WALL QUILTS
http://www.auntie.com/cnm/craftzine/joyquilt.htm

FLYING GEESE
FROM VIRGINIA CONSORTIUM OF QUILTERS
http://qqq.vcq.org
http://www.vcq.org/specialty%20lessons.htm/flying_geese.htm

SUNBONNET SUE CRIB QUILT
FROM KEEPSAKE QUILTING
http://www.keepsakequilting.com
http://www.keepsakequilting.com/html/sunbonnet_quilt.html

MARINER'S COMPASS FROM JUDY MATHIESON
http://members.aol.com/judy4quilt/MC1.html

STEP-BY-STEP BY GEORGIA BONESTEEL
http://www.georgiabonesteel.com/stepbystep.htm

Georgia offers a pattern for a 42" square sailboat quilt and a porpoise door warmer.

REFLECTIONS WALL QUILT BY JANET PAGE
http://www.benartex.com/reflections1.html

Complete instructions are available for the beautiful wallhanging Janet designed using Benartex fabrics.

TRIANGLE PIECE AND QUILT AS YOU GO
http://www.auntie.com/cnm/craftzine/triangleq.htm

DEBBY KRATOVIL EXPLAINS THREE DIMENSIONAL BOW TIES
http://www.kaper.org/queenb/bowtie.html

FREE WATERCOLOR QUILT PATTERN BY WHIMS
http://www.continet.com/whims
http://www.continet.com/whims/freeqp.html

CARD TRICK BABY QUILT
http://members.igateway.net/~jjanik/index.html

Instructions for making a machine-quilted baby quilt based on the card trick block.

12 DAYS OF CHRISTMAS LAP QUILT FROM QUILTWOMAN.COM
http://www.quiltwoman.com/12days.html

FOUR PATCH QUILT SAMPLER
http://www.press4success.com/SamplePlan.htm

DOUBLE DUTCH ROSE
http://piecebynumber.com/Sq/sqintro.htm

PINEAPPLE WALLHANGING FROM KAYE WOOD
http://www.kayewood.com/projectpg.html

"SPRING SPLASH," BY SHELBY MORRIS AND *McCALL'S QUILTING*
http://www.quickquilts.com/qquilts/golden/springsplash/pattern.htm

HAWAIIAN APPLIQUE CARNATION PATTERN BY CISSY SERANO
http://www.nvo.com/poakalani/files

COUNTRY SPICE QUILT PATTERN FROM THE GREAT AMERICAN QUILT FAMILY
http://www.possibilitiesquilt.com/freestuff.cfm

▦ Web Sites with Free Patterns for Other Quilted Goodies

PAT COULTER'S ONLINE COAT CLASS
http://woodstock.uplink.net/~coulter/coatclas.html

Instructions for stitching a quilted coat in African fabrics.

CATHEDRAL WINDOWS CUSHIONS FROM DY TAYLORS
http://www.tower.net.au/~fish/dycraft/cushion/cushion.html

QUILLOW PATTERN FROM DAWN DUPERAULT
http://www.reddawn.net/quilt/quillow.htm

A "quillow" is a cross between a pillow and quilt. It originated Down Under, just like a koala.

QUILTER'S HOT PACK FROM DAWN DUPERAULT
http://www.reddawn.net/quilt/hotpads.htm

A pattern for a hot or cold pack, just like the kind found in stores.

SCREENQUILT FROM KEEPSAKE QUILTING
http://www.keepsakequilting.com/html/screenquilt_.html

Directions for stitching up your own quilted computer cover, courtesy of quilting supplies catalog Keepsake Quilting.

When you tap into a pattern page don't forget to wait until the full page loads. "**Document done**" will flash on the bottom of your browser. Then use the scroll bars to scroll down to see the full page.

free Block-of-the-Month Clubs & Block Swaps

It's a simple concept: you stitch one block each month and before long you have enough for a quilt. Lots of Web sites feature an original monthly block pattern that you can download or print. Often these block-of-the-month clubs are organized around a theme (try appliquéd parrots). If you find a block-of-the-month series you like, bookmark it in your Web browser, then visit the Web site each month for a new pattern.

Block swaps are also popular with quilters on the Web. You stitch a stack of blocks in a theme—say, pieced dogs and cats— then swap them with other quilters. They mail you blocks that they've similarly stitched in the theme. It is a true cyber-quilter's bonding experience. For information on even more block swaps—and fabric ones, visit the big quilting Web sites in Chapter 4.

Free Block-of-the-Month Patterns

WORLD WIDE QUILTING PAGE'S BLOCK-OF-THE-MONTH
http://mail.kosmickitty.com/BlockOfTheMonth/BlockOfTheMonth98 99.html

DELPHI'S QUILTING ART BLOCK-OF-THE-MONTH
http://www.delphi.com/quilting

Select "Swaps and Activities" for the latest information.

ARTS AND QUILTS FREE BLOCK-OF-THE-MONTH
http://www.artsandquilts.com/free_patterns.htm

CRAZY QUILTERS BLOCK-OF-THE-MONTH
http://www.crazyquilters.com
http://www.crazyquilters.com/Patterns/BOM2000/bom2000.html

JO-ANN FABRICS' QUILTING
BLOCKS-OF-THE-MONTH
http://www.fabricenters.com/project/quilting

THE QUILT PATCH INTERNET NEWS
BLOCK-OF-THE-MONTH
http://www.quiltpatchva.com

JEANNE R. PRUE'S FLORAL BLOCKS-OF-THE-MONTH
http://www.jeanneraecrafts.com/quilt.html

SIMONE STRUSS' BLOCKS-OF-THE-MONTH
http://perso.wanadoo.fr/struss/bom/ebom.htm

QUILT CREATIONS BLOCK-OF-THE-MONTH
http://www.quiltcreations.com/summ.htm

QUILT BLOCK-OF-THE-MONTH FROM QUILT FRIENDS
http://www.quiltfriends.com/blockofmonth.html

MARY'S BLOCK-OF-THE-MONTH SERIES
http://www.totaldesignstudio.com/blocks

EQUILT.COM BLOCK-OF-THE-WEEK
http://www.equiltblocks.com

MINNESOTA QUILTERS' BLOCK-OF-THE-MONTH
http://www.mnquilt.org

SEW QUILTY'S BLOCK-OF-THE-MONTH
http://www.microserve.net/~jimwa3qy/sewquilty.html

FOUNDATION BLOCK-OF-THE-MONTH FROM BARBARA SKJØNBERG OF NORWAY
http://www.quilt-design.com/patindex.htm

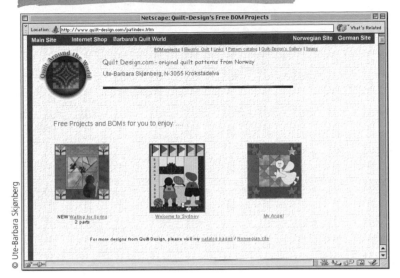

PATCHWORKS STUDIO—BLOCK-OF-THE-MONTH
http://www.patchworkstudio.com/blkmonth.htm

BLOCK-OF-THE-MONTH FROM QUILTTOWN USA
http://quilttownusa.com/Quilt_Shop/block.htm

JUDY MARTIN'S FREE BLOCK-OF-THE-MONTH
http://www.judymartin.com/bom/index.shtml

SCRAP QUILTS BLOCK-OF-THE-MONTH
http://www.scrapquilts.com

NEW LIFE CREATIONS BLOCK-OF-THE-MONTH
http://www.globnet.com/~flair/index.html

DEB KAUFFUNGER'S QUILTAHOLICS
BLOCK-OF-THE-MONTH
http://www.quiltaholics.com/projects.htm

© Quiltaholics, Holliston, MA

DOWNHOME QUILTING'S BLOCK-OF-THE-MONTH
http://downhomequilting.hypermart.net/bom.html

THIMBLENET BLOCK-OF-THE-MONTH
http://www.thimblenet.com/pattern_of_the_month.htm

Free Online Quilt Block Swaps

Now that you've got more quilt blocks than you know what to do with, how about swapping them with other quilters? These Web sites host regular block swaps.

SWAPS FROM QUILT FRIENDS
http://www.quiltfriends.com/swaps.html

WORLD WIDE QUILTERS TRADING POST
http://ttsw.com/TradingPost.html

BLOCK SWAPS AT QUILTERSBEE
http://www.quiltersbee.com/qbswaps.htm

DELPHI QUILTING FORUM SWAPS
http://www0.delphi.com/quilting/swaps9.html

MARY GRAHAM'S SWAPS AND EXHANGES PAGE
http://www.nmia.com/~mgdesign/qor/newswaps.html

QUILTCHAT'S FUNTASTIC BLOCK SWAPS
http://www.kathkwilts.com/swaps

NATIONAL ONLINE QUILTERS SWAPS
http://noqers.org

CRAZY QUILTERS BLOCK SWAPS
http://www.crazyquilters.com

QUILTER'S GARDEN SWAP LIST
http://www.periwinklekid.com/swap.htm

free Paper-Piecing Patterns & How-Tos

Paper piecing is easy. There are many different ways to do it. Some quilters iron freezer paper quilt pieces directly onto the back of their fabric. Others iron it onto the front of the fabric. There are different ways to draw the foundation patterns, too. You'll learn all about the different techniques on the Web sites we recommend in the first half of this chapter. Flip to the end of the chapter for our picks of the best free paper-piecing patterns on the Web.

Free Paper-Piecing How-Tos

CHRISTINE THRESH'S PAPER-PIECING PRIMER
http://www.winnowing.com/ppp.html

You'll find step-by-step instructions for learning paper piecing, or brushing up your skills.

PAPER PANACHE
http://www.paperpanache.com

• **HOW TO PAPER PIECE**
http://www.paperpanache.com/howto.htm

• **PAPER-PIECING FINE POINTS**
http://www.paperpanache.com/finepts.htm

• **UH, OH—MY BLOCK DOESN'T LIE FLAT**
http://www.paperpanache.com/laugh.htm

• **THE BUTTERFLY TRICK**
http://www.paperpanache.com/buttrfly.htm

A neat trick to help you cover any shape more easily.

PAPER-PIECING FROM CYNTHIA ENGLAND
http://www.englanddesign.com/sample/engine1b.htm
http://www.englanddesign.com/sample/engine1.htm

*Cynthia shares her techniques for sewing precision-pieced blocks with freezer paper ironed to the front of the fabric. There are cutting and sewing directions, and tips on how to realign pattern pieces if their seams don't fall right. Visit Cynthia's gallery (**http://www.englanddesign.com/ gallery/gallery1.htm**) to see her award-winning quilts.*

FOUNDATION PAPER-PIECING— PARTS ONE AND TWO BY SUSAN C. DRUDING AND ABOUT.COM
http://quilting.about.com/hobbies/quilting/library/weekly/ aa070797.htm
http://quilting.about.com/hobbies/quilting/library/weekly/ aa071697.htm

Susan explains how to sew simple as well as complex foundation blocks. She offers free patterns and other resources.

FOUNDATION PIECING FROM QUILTTOWN USA
http://quilttownusa.com/Quilt_Shop/fpbeginners1a.htm

Texas quiltmaker Miriam Neuringer explains how to stitch to a marked foundation pattern.

BASIC FOUNDATION PIECING FROM QUILTMAKER
http://www.quiltmaker.com/qm/tech/tech8.htm

NO MORE SLIPPED PIECES
FROM PIECE BY NUMBER
http://www.piecebynumber.com/dn/dntip1.htm

Here's a good assortment of tips for correctly aligning and sewing oddly shaped pieces of fabric to a foundation base.

HOW TO PAPER PIECE BY DAVID SMALL
http://www.small-expressions.com/instruct/howto.htm

ENGLISH PAPER-PIECING BY DAVID SMALL
http://www.small-expressions.com/instruct/text12.htm

FREEZER PAPER-PIECING LESSON
BY ELSIE VREDENBURG
http://users.netonecom.net/~elf/cardinal.htm

HOW TO BASTE ENGLISH PAPER-PIECING SHAPES
BY CD DESIGNS
http://home.flash.net/~cddesign/PaperPiecing/how.htm

FOUNDATION BLOCK PIECING
FROM THE WORLD WIDE QUILTING PAGE
http://www.quilt.com/HowTo/FoundationHowToPage.html

FOUNDATION PAPER-PIECING
FROM MARY GRAHAM
http://www.nmia.com/~mgdesign/qor/technique/pfp.htm

DEBRA WEISS' "OUTRAGEOUS FOUNDATION
PIECING" FROM QUILT GALLERY MAGAZINE
http://www.quiltgallery.com/technique1.htm

FOUNDATION/PAPER-PIECING LESSONS
FROM ZIPPY DESIGNS
http://www.zippydesigns.com/Lessons/lessonsindex.html

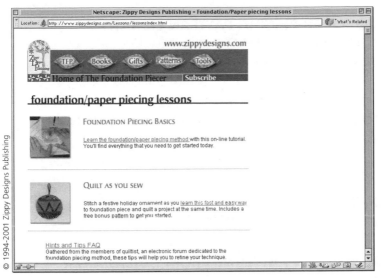

You'll find an illustrated tutorial for paper-piecing, instructions for a "quilt as you go" method of piecing, and a collection of hints and tips.

CUTTING ODD ANGLES IN FOUNDATION PIECING
http://www.geocities.com/pcpiecers/goofyangletips.html

FREE BLOCK HOW-TOS FROM MY TIME
http://www.mytimepatterns.com/basics.html

▦ Free Paper-Piecing Patterns

QUILT TALK PAPER-PIECING PATTERNS
http://www.quilttalk.com/paperpiece/pp.html

FOUNDATION BLOCKS
FROM THE WORLD WIDE QUILT PAGE
http://www.quilt.com/Foundations/Foundations.html

DEBBY KRATOVIL'S QUILTER BY DESIGN
http://www.kaper.org/queenb
http://www.kaper.org/queenb/pc.patterns.html

FREE PAPER-PIECING PATTERN LIBRARY FROM ZIPPY DESIGNS
http://www.zippydesigns.com/Library/libraryindex.html

FOUNDATION BLOCK PATTERNS FROM DAVID SMALL'S SMALL EXPRESSIONS
http://small-expressions.com/patterns/patterns.htm

Small Expressions offers 40 free foundation block patterns.

FOUNDATION-PIECING
http://members.aol.com/heart2hnd/Piecing.html

FOUNDATION PATTERNS FROM *QUILTMAKER*
http://www.quiltmaker.com/qm/patterns/patt7.htm

FOUNDATION BLOCK PATTERNS FROM DAVID SMALL
http://small-expressions.com/patterns/patterns.htm

FOUNDATION-PIECING ARCHIVE
http://members.aol.com/heart2hnd/Archive.html

FOUNDATION-PIECED SANTA FROM CRAFTY ROSE
http://www.craftyrose.com/santa.htm

FREE PATTERNS FROM SUNSHINE QUILTERS
http://sunshineguild.hypermart.net/patterns.htm

FLYING GEESE IN A CIRCLE
BY CARYL BRYER FALLERT
http://www.bryerpatch.com/pattern/pattern.htm

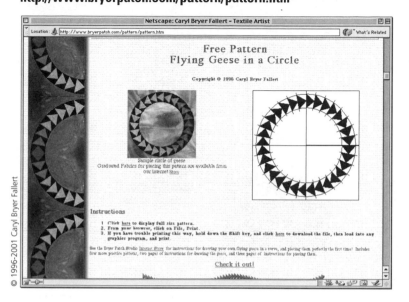

© 1996-2001 Caryl Bryer Fallert

ORIENTAL TEA GARDEN VEST FROM CAROL DOAK
http://www.patchwork.com/recroom/FreeVest.htm

FREE CHRISTMAS BLOCKS
FROM QUILT SEEDS DESIGNS
http://www.quiltseeds.com/christmas_block_patterns.htm

PATTERNS FROM CHRISTINE THRESH
http://www.winnowing.com/patterns.html

Scroll to the bottom of the page for a pattern for a morning glory, daisy, piece of cake, a baby chick and eggs, and other cute patterns.

FREE PAPER-PIECING PATTERNS AND PROJECTS FROM PATCHPIECES BY PATTI R. ANDERSON
http://www.patchpieces.com/Paperpiece.html

Patti shares her original patterns, including one for butterflies, a star heart ornament, and other designs. You need Adobe Acrobat to view them.

FREE BLOCKS FROM QUILT SEEDS DESIGNS
http://www.quiltseeds.com/Blocks.htm

PIECE BY NUMBER
http://piecebynumber.com
http://piecebynumber.com/pastbom/archbom.htm

CHAPTER 9
free Mystery Quilt Projects

Mystery quilts are popular among quilters on the Web. The idea is that the quilter follows cutting and assembly instructions on a Web site to assemble a quilt without knowing in advance what the finished quilt will look like. That is assuming that the quilter doesn't "skip ahead" to view the last installment of the mystery, if all the episodes are posted. The cutting and stitching instructions are often accompanied by installments of a mystery story on the Web site.

Some mystery quilt projects run as long as a year, with participants tapping into the site each month for new assembly instructions. Here are Web sites where you'll find mystery quilt projects, stories—and fellow quilting mystery lovers.

MYSTERY QUILTS FROM ZIPPY DESIGNS
http://www.zippydesigns.com/Library/libraryindex.html

- **PEACE ON EARTH**
http://www.zippydesigns.com/Library/PeaceOnEarth/POE.html

- **SPRING TREATS**
http://www.zippydesigns.com/Library/SpringTreats/SpringTreats.html

- **NATURE'S BOUNTY**
http://www.zippydesigns.com/Library/NaturesBounty/NBounty.html

MYSTERY QUILT IN FOUR PARTS BY TRICIA REVEST
http://members.tripod.co.uk/London_Quilters/mystery.htm

TIP For links to additional mystery quilts, see **Sewn by Joan, Mystery Quilt Links** (**http://www.dragonbbs.com/members/1217/mystery.htm**) and **The Quilt Channel's Mysteries** (**http://www.quiltchannel.com/Fun/mysteries.htm**).

DUTCHMAN DESIGNS'
FREE MYSTERY QUILT PATTERNS
http://www.dutdes.com/ddfree.html

Jo and Jos Hindriks share mystery quilt block patterns complete with detective stories. If you're wondering what the puzzle Pentominoes can do for your quilt, this site also includes designs featuring puzzling patterns. One of their mystery quilt projects is for an especially cute cat quilt.

THE MYSTERY PAGE FROM QUILT SEEDS DESIGNS
http://www.quiltseeds.com/mystery.htm

A MYSTERY FROM THE QUILT PATCH
http://www.quiltpatchva.com/MysteryQuilt/mystery.htm#Mystery

PATCHWORK MYSTERY BY DIAN "E/LESS" MOORE
http://people.delphi.com/quiltnsew/eless.html

MYSTERY QUILTS BY PEG BENNETT,
FROM AUNTIE.COM
http://auntie.com/qzine/mysterymain.asp

Peg shares two mystery quilts, Twisted Tales (hint: meow!) and Lucky Star.

PAPER PANACHE
http://www.paperpanache.com

Tune in each month to obtain a free mystery block destined to result in a lovely quilt. Past mystery blocks are available for a small fee online. They are beauties!

NATIONAL ONLINE QUILTERS—QUILT DECTECTIVE
http://noqers.org/mysteries/mystqilt.html

Tune in every two weeks for another clue until you solve the "quilt mystery."

SUNBONNET SLEUTH MYSTERY QUILTS
http://www.quilttalk.com/SunBSleuth.html

PLANET PATCHWORK MYSTERY
http://www.planetpatchwork.com/mystery.htm

MARCUS BROTHERS' MYSTERY QUILT
http://www.marcusbrothers.com/mystery_quilt/index.shtml

A MYSTERY FROM THE QUILT PATCH
AND LESLIE A. PFEIFER & ANN C. POOL
http://www.quiltpatchva.com/MysteryQuilt/mystery.htm

MYSTERY QUILTS FROM NEW LIFE CREATIONS
http://www.globnet.com/~flair/index.html

STAINED GLASS MYSTERY QUILT FROM QUILTAHOLICS
http://www.quiltaholics.com/mystery.htm

LE QUILT MYSTÈRE DE FRANCE-PATCHWORK
FROM MARIE-NOÎLLE GELAS
http://francepatchwork.com/quilt_mystere.htm

COUNTDOWN TO CHRISTMAS
http://www.mountain-inter.net/~graham/xmasintr.html

MITER SHE WROTE—
JESSICA FOUR-PATCH'S CASE #108
http://quilt.com/Mystery108/Mystery108Part1.html

The World Wide Quilting Page and Schoolhouse Enterprises share a pattern for a gorgeous mystery quilt from Merry May.

QUILTS: NOT JUST FOR BEDS—
MYSTERY QUILTER #4 BY JANE L. KAKALEY
http://www.eskimo.com/~jlk/mystery4.htm

We peeked at the photo of this mystery quilt, and it's a beauty!

PAT COULTER'S MYSTERY QUILTS 1 AND 2
http://woodstock.uplink.net/~coulter/star.html
http://woodstock.uplink.net/~coulter/myst1.html

PATCHPIECES PUZZLER QUILT
http://www.patchpieces.com/BytebyByte.html

MYSTERY QUILTS FROM ROSIE'S CALICO CUPBOARD
http://www.rosiescalicocupboard.com

Scroll toward the bottom of the page for the current mystery quilt and links to past mystery projects.

DOWN HOME QUILTING'S MYSTERY PAGE
http://downhomequilting.hypermart.net/mystery.html

T!P

Looking for the Literature-Quilt Connection? Head to **Betty Reynolds' Quilts, Quilters, Quilting, and Patchwork in Adult Fiction** (**http://www.nmt.edu/~breynold/quiltfiction_adult.html**) and **Quilts, Quilters, Quilting, and Patchwork in Fiction for Children and Young Adults** (**http://www.nmt.edu/~breynold/quiltfiction_kids.html**) for lists of fiction that includes quilt themes and references.

INSPECTOR CLUESEW: NO STRINGS ATTACHED, COURTESY OF ROB HOLLAND & QUILTROPOLIS
http://www.quiltchannel.com/strippy.htm

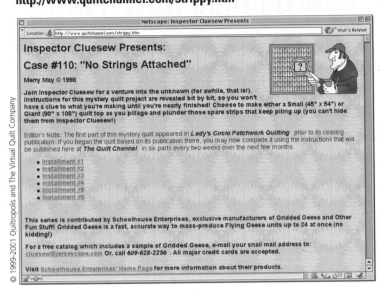

C2C MYSTERY QUILTERS' PAGE
http://members.aol.com/Quilters2/quiltershp.htm

MYSTERY QUILT
FROM MARCUS BROTHERS TEXTILES, INC.
http://marcusbrothers.com/mystery_quilt/index.shtml

QUILTER'S NEIGHBORHOOD MYSTERY QUILTERS
http://www.mountain-inter.net/~graham/mystery.html

QUILTAHOLICS MYSTERY QUILT
http://www.quiltaholics.com/mystery.htm

QUILT BUS MYSTERY QUILT
http://www.quiltbus.com/Mystery%20Quilt.htm

ELECTRIC QUILT'S MYSTERY QUILT
http://www.electricquilt.com/mystery/index.html

free Quilting How-Tos

Our great-grandmothers taught quilting in kitchens and parlors. Wouldn't they be surprised to learn that one day their techniques would be taught on computers and spread around the world via phone lines and something called the Internet? You can find literally thousands of quilting how-tos on the Web—directions for making Dresden Plate blocks, drawing eight-point stars, stitching needle-turn appliqué, or getting a quilt to lie flat. You'll even find advice on how to hand-quilt.

Here are some of our favorite quilting how-to Web sites. By the time you read this there will surely be many more.

Free Basic Quilting How-tos

DAWN DUPERAULT'S
FREQUENTLY ASKED QUILTING QUESTIONS
http://www.reddawn.net/quilt/quilting.htm

Dawn provides answers to all the most basic questions, from how to start your quilting hobby to how to find quilting guilds online.

LESSONS FROM *McCALLS QUILTING*
http://www.mccallsquilting.com/qquilts/lessons/index.htm

Quilting Fundamentals includes lessons in appliqué, backing, basting, marking, rotary cutting, pressing, hand and machine quilting, templates, and more. A glossary of quilting terms and a step-by-step rotary cutting guide are included.

QUILTING BASICS FROM *THE QUILTER* MAGAZINE
http://www.thequiltermag.com/basics.html

THE CRANSTON VILLAGE QUILT SHOP
http://www.cranstonvillage.com/quilt/q-lesson.htm

The fabric maker offers lessons on getting started quilting, purchasing fabric, cutting and marking templates, sewing, finishing, and more.

QUILTING LESSONS FROM *QUILT MAGAZINE*
http://www.quiltmag.com/lessons.html

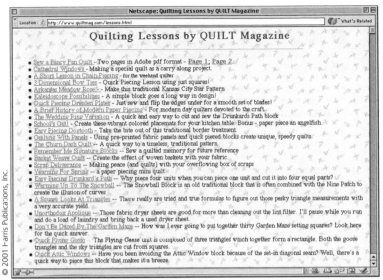

You'll find plenty of lessons here, including ones for quick-piecing Dresden Plates, quilting with panels, making basket weave quilts, quick flying geese, and more.

TEN BASIC LESSONS FROM KWIK SQUARES
http://www.mwaz.com/quilt/00_toc.htm

Kwik Squares, of Prescott Valley, Arizona, offers lessons in quilting, block assembly, stitching, sashings, borders, notions, battings, and more.

QUILT USA—LESSONS
http://quilttownusa.com/Quilt_Shop/beginners.htm

How-tos include ones on how to sew a dimensional bow-tie quilt, creating a hanging sleeve, two-fabric binding for reversible quilts, hand quilting basics, and more.

RITA DENENBERG'S QUILTING HOW-TOS
http://myquilts.hypermart.net/projects.htm

Rita shows you how to make continuous tube bias binding, how to master freezer paper appliqué, miter corners, square off blocks and quilts, make your own border pattern, prairie points, and more.

© 2001 Harris Publications, Inc.

#QUILTCHAT IRC CHANNEL QUILT LESSONS
http://kathkwilts.com/lessons

You don't have to tap into an Internet chat channel to read the quilting techniques shared by members of Kathy Somers' #QuiltChat channel. Lessons include: How to build a floor frame, Dresden Plate directions, mastering borders, and more.

CRAZY QUILTER'S LESSONS
http://www.crazyquilters.com

Read "Quilter's Info" for stitching a crazy quilt, tips, a chart of standard quilt sizes, and instructions for making continuous bias.

MAKING QUILTS AND COMFORTERS
FROM MOUNTAIN MIST
http://www.stearnstextiles.com/mountainmist/tutor/tutor1.htm

PRESSING AND HOW-TO BASICS
FROM MYRNA GIESBRECHT
http://www.press4success.com/HowTo.htm

Download free lessons on pressing basics, drawing a box grid to stitch half-square triangles, rotary cutting basics, connector corners, and binding basics. Adobe Acrobat required.

QUILT SCHOOL FROM QUILT FRIENDS
http://www.quiltfriends.com/quiltschool.html

BASICS FROM QUILTER'S VILLAGE.COM
http://www.quiltersvillage.com/basic1.htm

Tutorials are geared for the beginner and include ones on marking templates, cutting, how to make double-fold binding, and sewing a sleeve for hanging a quilt.

QUILT STYLES FROM MARY GRAHAM
http://www.nmia.com/~mgdesign/qor/styles/styles.htm

Mary explains different styles of quilting, including Amish, Hawaiian, and southwestern, and offers patterns and tips

JUDY MARTIN'S CLASSROOM
http://www.judymartin.com/classroom/index.shtml

Judy offers guides to binding, tricks for quilting with toddlers underfoot, cutting half-trapezoids and 45-degree diamonds, and class outlines for teaching her patterns.

LUCY FAZELY'S EDUCATIONAL HANDOUTS
http://www.lucyfazely.com/howto/index.htm

Lucy tells you how to make templates for machine or hand appliqué, how to piece your quilt top, and how to identify quilt blocks.

Free Drafting, Template, and Piecing How-tos

A SQUARE LOOKS AT TRIANGLES
BY DEBBY KRATOVIL
http://www.quiltmag.com/lessons/square.triangles.html

JUDY MARTIN'S SHORT STRIPS:
BETTER, FASTER ROTARY CUTTING
http://ttsw.com/Artists/JudyMartin/ShortStrips.html

DRAFTING 101 FROM JAN P. KRENTZ
http://JanKrentz.com
http://home.att.net/~jpkrentz/freelesson.html

PAT COULTER'S ONLINE FRIGID PIECING CLASS FOR PIECING QUILTS WITH IRREGULAR AND THREE-DIMENSIONAL SHAPES
http://woodstock.uplink.net/~coulter/frclass.html

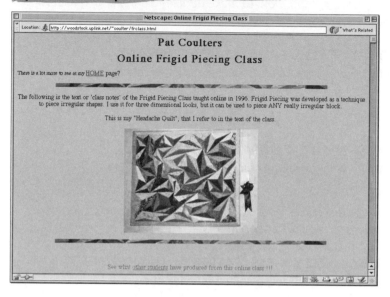

KALEIDOSCOPE: BEYOND-THE-BLOCK DESIGNS FROM QUILTING TECHNIQUES, INC.
http://www.quiltingtechniquesinc.com/kaldesign.html

HOW TO FIGURE YARDAGE FOR RIGHT TRIANGLES
http://www.gotomywebpage.com/quiltdesigns/yardtri.htm

HOW TO FIGURE YARDAGE FOR SQUARES
http://www.gotomywebpage.com/quiltdesigns/yardsq.htm

FAST CUT SEWING TIPS
http://www.gotomywebpage.com/quiltdesigns/fastcut.htm

HOW TO MEASURE—YARDAGE CONVERSION
http://www.gotomywebpage.com/quiltdesigns/measure.htm

MAKING YOUR OWN TEMPLATES BY CANDY GOFF
http://www.handquilter.com/html/august97tip.html

"PIECING CURVES WITHOUT GOING AROUND THE BEND" BY JOANNA BARNES
http://wso.williams.edu/~jbarnes/quilting/curves.htm

DAVID SMALL SHOWS YOU HOW TO DRAFT AN EIGHT-POINTED STAR
http://www.small-expressions.com/instruct/text3b.htm

QUILT DESIGN TEMPLATES BY MARY GRAHAM
http://www.nmia.com/~mgdesign/qor/pattern/quilttemplates/
  quilttemplate.htm

JINNY BEYER TEACHES SOFT EDGE PIECING
http://www.jinnybeyer.com/tips/tip02-1.cfm

PIECING ALIGNMENTS BY MARY GRAHAM
http://www.nmia.com/~mgdesign/qor/begin/align.htm

QUILT BORDERS BY KATHKWILTS
http://www.quiltchat.com/lessons/borders.html

QUICK PIECING HALF SQUARE TRIANGLES BY MARY GRAHAM
http://www.nmia.com/~mgdesign/qor/technique/hst.htm

Y-SEAM FREE LESSON FROM JAN P. KRENTZ
http://JanKrentz.com
http://home.att.net/~jpkrentz/yseams_public.htm

MARINER'S COMPASS CONSTRUCTION BY KATHERINE SPRAGGINS
http://members.tripod.com/~kspragg/marhome/marhome.htm

BORDER STRATEGIES FROM CANDY GOFF
http://www.handquilter.com/html/april99tip.html

QUILT DRAFTING
FROM THE WORLD WIDE QUILTING PAGE
http://mail.kosmickitty.com/HowTo/Drafting.html

SPEED PIECING BASICS
FROM THE WORLD WIDE QUILTING PAGE
http://mail.kosmickitty.com/HowTo/SpeedPiecingDirections.html

 *Free Border How-tos*

PRAIRIE POINT BORDERS BY MARY GRAHAM
http://www.nmia.com/~mgdesign/qor/technique/prpnts.htm

JINNY BEYER EXPLAINS PLANNING A BORDER
http://www.jinnybeyer.com/tips/tip14.cfm

JINNY BEYER SHOWS YOU HOW TO USE BORDERS
http://www.jinnybeyer.com/blocks/main07.html

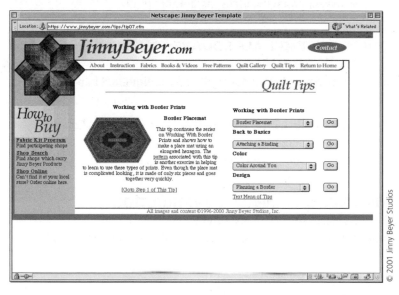

"EASY PIECING DOGTOOTH BORDERS" FROM *QUILT MAGAZINE*

http://www.quiltmag.com/lessons/dogtooth/dogtooth.html

"JOANNA'S MIGHTY SUSPECT MAGIC MITERING METHOD" BY JOANNA BARNES

http://wso.williams.edu/~jbarnes/quilting/mit_hard.htm

 Free Appliqué How-tos

DAVID SMALL EXPLAINS MACHINE APPLIQUÉ SATIN STITCH

http://www.small-expressions.com/instruct/text14.htm

CRITTER PATTERN WORKS MACHINE APPLIQUÉ LESSON

http://www.critterpat.com/back2basics.html

STEP-BY-STEP GUIDE TO QUICK APPLIQUÉ FROM QTOONS

http://www.qtoons.com
http://www.qtoons.com/steps/step1.htm

HAND APPLIQUÉ, FREEZER PAPER APPLIQUÉ, AND MACHINE APPLIQUÉ WITH FUSIBLE WEB INSTRUCTIONS FROM QUILT CREATIONS IN FRANCE

http://www.quiltcreations.com/eng/applique.htm

MARY GRAHAM'S FREEZER PAPER METHOD, CLIP AND BASTE METHOD, AND NEEDLE-TURN AND REVERSE APPLIQUÉ

http://www.nmia.com/~mgdesign/qor/begin/applique.htm

LESLIE LEVISON'S CRAZY QUILT
PATCHWORK BLOCK ONLINE CLASS—PART ONE
http://www.caron-net.com/classes/classmayfiles/clasmay1.html

LESLIE LEVISON'S CRAZY QUILT
PATCHWORK BLOCK ONLINE CLASS—PART TWO
http://www.caron-net.com/classes/classmayfiles/clasmay2.html

CD DESIGNS' "HOW TO APPLIQUÉ
A HEART WITH FREEZER PAPER"
http://www.flash.net/~cddesign/FreezerPaper/How-Applique.htm

"APPLIQUÉ, THE 'A' WORD SIMPLIFIED" BY ADDY
HARKAVY FROM *QUILT GALLERY MAGAZINE*
http://www.quiltgallery.com/technique3.htm

DAVID SMALL EXPLAINS
HAND BUTTONHOLE APPLIQUÉ
http://www.small-expressions.com/instruct/text13.htm

APPLIQUÉ ANGEL LESSON FROM WARM & NATURAL
http://www.warmcompany.com/angel.html

APPLIQUÉ TIPS FROM QUILT CREATIONS
http://www.quiltcreations.com/eng/applique.htm

APPLIQUÉ AND ENGLISH PIECING
FROM QUILTING TECHNIQUES, INC.
http://www.quiltingtechniquesinc.com/lesson.html

MAKE A MOLA
http://www.conexus.si.edu/kuna/eng/make_mola

HOW TO MAKE A MOLA
BY APPLIQUÉ EXPERT CHARLOTTE PATERA
http://www.jps.net/patera/modress.html

INVISIBLE MACHINE APPLIQUÉ USING
ADJUSTABLE ZIPPER FOOT BY SHARLA HICKS
http://www.softexpressions.com/help/faq/faqmachappliq.html

Free Hand and Machine Quilting How-tos

HAND QUILTING TIPS FROM QUILTNET, COURTESY OF WORLD WIDE QUILTING PAGE
http://ttsw.com/HowTo/HandQuiltingHowTo.html

HAND QUILTING TIPS FROM *THREADS*
http://www.taunton.com/th/features/techniques/th93knot_stori.htm

"THIRTY WAYS TO IMPROVE YOUR QUILTING," FROM *QUILTER'S NEWSLETTER MAGAZINE*
http://www.quiltersnewsletter.com/qnm/feature5.htm

CARYL FALLERT'S TIPS ON MACHINE QUILTING
http://www.bryerpatch.com/faq/mq.htm

QUILT IT FREEHAND BY JOE CUNNINGHAM FROM *THREADS*
http://www.taunton.com/th/features/design/quiltfree/1.htm

CANDY GOFF'S HANDQUILTER PAGE
http://www.handquilter.com

Candy pieces and quilts her quilts entirely by hand, and on her Web site shares her special methods. Tips include estimating how long it will take to quilt and a multiple needle technique for hand quilting.

TYING A QUILT BY MARY GRAHAM
http://www.nmia.com/~mgdesign/qor/begin/tying.htm

TYING A QUILT BY HEDDI CRAFT
http://www.thecraftstudio.com/qwc/finish.htm

Free Quilt Binding and Finishing How-tos

AVOIDING WAVY EDGES
FROM WIDE WORLD QUILTING PAGE
http://ttsw.com/FAQS/WavyEdgesFAQ.html

SMOOTH JOIN ON QUILT BINDING FROM THREADS
http://www.taunton.com/th/features/techniques/39quilt.htm

JULIE COGHILL SHARES HER BINDING TIPS
http://www2.polarnet.com/~rcoghill/binding.html

HOW TO MAKE A HANGING SLEEVE FOR A QUILT FROM MARY GRAHAM DESIGNS
http://www.nmia.com/~mgdesign/qor/technique/hang.htm

RITA DENENBERG EXPLAINS HOW TO MAKE CONTINUOUS TUBE BIAS BINDING
http://myquilts.hypermart.net/tubebind.htm

CAROLYN'S FAVORITE EDGE BINDING FOR QUILTS AND FINISHING A CORNER WITH CUT STRIPS
http://www.clark.net/pub/quilters/library/geninfo.htm

HOW TO FIX BINDING TROUBLES
http://www.quiltcreations.com/eng/binding.htm

FINISHING A QUILT—EDGES AND LABELS BY HEDDI CRAFT
http://www.thecraftstudio.com/qwc/finish.htm

More free Quilting Tips

A ll the big quilting Web sites we recommend in Chapter 4 feature lots of quilting tips and tutorials. Quilting magazines and vendors of quilting tools, books and patterns also offer regular tips on their Web sites. Here are a few more Web sites worth bookmarking that offer regular collections of quilting advice collected from quilters on the Web.

SUE TRAUDT'S WORLD WIDE QUILTING PAGE HOW-TOS
http://ttsw.com/HowToPage.html

You'll find lots and lots of advice here about block and foundation piecing, rotary cutting, speed cutting, appliqué, hand and machine quilting, bindings, basting, and more. Take a look at the following World Wide Quilting pages, too:

- **THE WORLD WIDE QUILTING PAGE'S HINTS**
http://quilt.com/Hints.html
- **THE WORLD WIDE QUILTING PAGE'S MISCELLANEOUS HELP**
http://ttsw.com/MiscQuiltingPage.html
- **THE NATIONAL ONLINE QUILTERS TIPS AND LESSONS**
http://www.noqers.org/tips/tips.shtml

TIPS AND TECHNIQUES FROM QUILTMAKER
http://www.quiltmaker.com/qm/tips.htm

FUTURE HEIRLOOMS HINTS AND HUMOR
http://www.future-heirlooms.com/pages/hints00.html

PATCHWORK STUDIOS HINTS AND TIPS
http://www.patchworkstudio.com/lesson1.htm

TIPS AND TRICKS FROM QUILTS LIMITED
http://www.quiltslimited.com/Tips.html

TAP INTO THE USENET TEXTILE FAQS FOR ANSWERS

The Usenet FAQs are famous compilations of advice that has been posted over the years in the newsgroups **alt.sewing** and the **rec.crafts.textile** ones. They include quilting advice as well as lots of general sewing advice. They're updated monthly, and you'll find them posted all over the Web, including in each of the newsgroups each month.

TEXTILES PART 1 OF 2—FAQ
ftp://rtfm.mit.edu/pub/usenet/news.answers/crafts/
textiles/faq/part1

TEXTILES PART 2 OF 2—FAQ
ftp://rtfm.mit.edu/pub/usenet/news.answers/crafts/
textiles/faq/part2

TEXTILE RELATED BOOKS PART 1 OF 3—FAQ
ftp://rtfm.mit.edu/pub/usenet/news.answers/crafts/
textiles/books/part1

TEXTILE RELATED BOOKS PART 2 OF 3—FAQ
ftp://rtfm.mit.edu/pub/usenet/news.answers/crafts/
textiles/books/part2

TEXTILE RELATED BOOKS PART 3 OF 3—FAQ
ftp://rtfm.mit.edu/pub/usenet/news.answers/crafts/
textiles/books/part3

MICHIANA FREE-NET FAQ ABOUT SEWING
http://michiana.org/MFNetLife/SewingFAQ.html

THE SEWING FAQ
http://www.skepsis.com/~tfarrell/textiles/sewing/faq.html

By Tom Farrell and Paulo Ruffino with contributions from the readers of alt.sewing and rec.crafts.textiles.sewing.

YOUR FREQUENTLY ASKED QUESTIONS ANSWERED BY DAWN DUPERAULT
http://www.reddawn.net/quilt/quilting.htm

AMERICA QUILTS TIPS & TECHNIQUES
http://www.pbs.org/americaquilts/tips/index.html

CANDY GOFF'S TIP ARCHIVE
http://www.handquilter.com/html/tipsarchive.html

TIPS FROM QUILTERS UNLIMITED MEMBERS
http://www.clark.net/pub/quilters/library/tipmem.htm

NEEDLEWORK TIPS AND TRICKS FROM MARTHA BETH LEWIS'S PIANO, NEEDLEWORK & CHOCOLATE HOME PAGE
http://www.serve.com/marbeth/tips.html

Interested in taking a quilting class but reluctant to leave the comfort of your computer? Tap into **Quilt University** (**http://www.quiltuniversity.com**) where you can enroll in a variety of for-fee quilting classes on topics ranging from piecing to appliqué, to surface embellishment, dyeing, color and design, computer quilting, and foundation piecing. A free sample class is available

🐝 QUILTING TIPS FROM JINNY BEYER STUDIO
http://www.jinnybeyer.com/quilttips.cfm

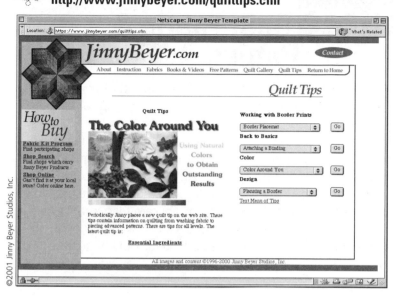

QUILT BUS QUILT TIPS AND TERMS
http://www.quiltbus.com/Quilt%20Terms.htm

TIP OF THE WEEK ARCHIVE
FROM FONS AND PORTER
http://www.fonsandporter.com/tipoftheweekarchive.html

QUILTING TIPS BY SREGORA
FROM TERRY CRAWFORD PIERCE
http://www.sregora.com/quilting/sregora/quilttips.html

QUILTING TIPS FROM QUILTAHOLICS
http://www.quiltaholics.com/tips.htm

DOWN UNDER QUILTERS' TIPS PAGE
http://www.duquilts.com.au/office/helppage.htm

TIPS & TECHNIQUES FROM KAYE WOOD
http://www.kayewood.com/tips.html

free Quilt Fabric & Batting Advice

Remember that first quilt you made—stitched of polyester doubleknit from your dad's leisure suit, and snips of wool from your sister's school uniform? Don't tell us that since then you haven't become a bit of, well, a fabric snob. You buy fabric like some buy designer purses, looking for names of designers like Nancy Crow and Jinny Beyer. You indulge in lengthy conversations on the best thread count for muslin. You mull over the properties of different brands of batting with more care than most people expend shopping for a house. If this sounds like you, you're going to love the Internet. That's because there are lots of quilters on it who devote as much passion as you do to shopping for fabric— and they are always eager to share their opinions.

Free Fabric Advice

The best fabric advice you'll find on the Web will come from other quilters. **Quiltropolis (http://www.quiltropolis.net/maillists/maillists.asp)** runs a mailing list discussion group called FabricFind & Facts. It's devoted to discussing fiber care, trends in fabrics, and selecting the proper fabric for sewing projects. Judith Gridley is the moderator. They run another discussion group called VintageFabrics, run by Joan Kiplinger. It's devoted to the use and appreciation of fabrics from another time. A third mailing list, Asia Threads, focuses on the appreciation and acquisition of fabrics with Asian roots.

Try Out Your Fabrics on Virtual Design Tables Before Buying Them Several Web sellers of fabric offer "virtual design tables" in which you can group together swatches from their Web site's inventory to see how they will look together. Head to: **Connecting Threads (http://www.connectingthreads.com)**; eQuilter **(http://www.oquilter.com)**; and Lunn Fabrics **(http://www.lunnfabrics.com)**.

You'll get lots of fabric advice from quilters in other mailing lists too. Head to Chapter 3 for directions on how to tap into the lists.

The QuiltNet mailing list maintains some of the best collections of fabric advice on the Net. Here are the addresses where you can tap in:

QUILTNET BLEEDING FABRIC FAQ
http://ttsw.com/FAQS/BleedingFabricFAQ.htm

This is a compilation of suggestions on dealing with and preventing fabric bleeding. It comes courtesy of Sue Traudt's World Wide Quilting web site.

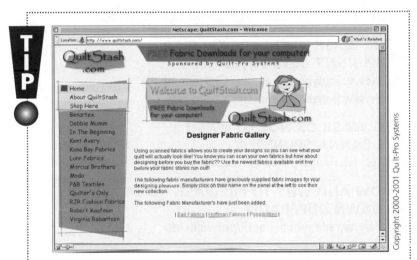

Download the Latest Fabric Swatches from Your Favorite Manufacturer in Digital Format! At Quilt Stash.Com (**http://www.quiltstash.com**) you can view and download the latest fabric swatches from your favorite manufacturers, including Kona Bay, RJR, Benartex, and others. You can view the fabrics in sample quilt blocks and quilt designs. This wonderful free service is provided by Quilt-Pro Systems. To save fabric swatches to disk right-click on the block and select Save as... from the pop-up menu. The swatches are in the GIF graphics format, and can be used with Quilt-Pro and 1-2-3 Quilt! quilt design software. You can convert them to other graphics formats with any graphics program.

FABRIC STORAGE FAQ
http://www.quilt.com/FAQS/FabricStorageFAQ.html

This is a compilation of advice from QuiltNet on how to store fabric. It also comes courtesy of Sue Traudt's World Wide Quilting.

QUILTERSBEE FABRIC TIPS
http://www.quiltersbee.com/qbfabtip.htm

Here's a selection of tips collected from the mailing list group QuiltersBee and compiled by Addy Harkavy.

• MANAGING YOUR FABRIC STASH
BY CANDY GOFF
http://www.handquilter.com/html/september97tip.html

• THE WASH AND CARE FABRICS
FROM JINNY BEYER STUDIOS
http://www.jinnybeyer.com/tips/tip01a.html
http://www.jinnybeyer.com/tips/tip01b.cfm

• TO WASH OR NOT TO WASH
BY DEANNA SPINGOLA
http://www.spingola.com/prewash.htm

• HOW AND WHY TO PREWASH YOUR FABRIC
BY DAWN DUPERAULT
http://www.reddawn.net/quilt/prewash.htm

FABRIC ADVICE
FROM THE UNIVERSITY OF NEBRASKA EXTENSION
http://www.ianr.unl.edu/PUBS/textiles

UNL offers a library of articles on fabric selection, use, and care, many by Rose Marie Tondle. Topics include: preparing fabric for sewing, sewing on denim, stain and mildew removal advice, removing skunk odors, moth protection, stain removal advice, textile conservation, and more.

CRANSTON PRINT WORKS'
A BEGINNER'S GUIDE TO FABRICS
http://www.cranstonvillage.com/library/l-f-fabg.htm

Learn how to select fabrics, and learn the difference between fabrics like cambric and chambray, broadcloth and chino.

FABRIC ADVICE FROM OHIO STATE UNIVERSITY
http://www.ag.ohio-state.edu/~ohioline/lines/home.html

OSU also offers an extensive library of articles on fabric, many authored by Joyce A. Smith and Barbara Scruggs. Topics include: sewing on rayon and microfibers, proper placement of fabric for machine stitching, cleaning fabrics contaminated with pesticides, how to deal with fabric staining by iron in the water, and fabric care labeling.

Web Sites of Major Quilting Fabric Makers

Many fabric makers run Web sites where you can find information on their fabric lines, free patterns, a database of stores that carry different lines (a big help when you're trying to locate specific fabric), general fabric advice, and in some cases even message areas where you can search for other quilters who may have an extra quarter of that discontinued fabric you need to finish your quilt.

BALI FABRICS
http://www.balifab.com

BENARTEX QUILT FABRICS
http://www.benartex.com

CRANSTON PRINT WORKS (HOME OF VIP FABRICS)
http://www.cranstonvillage.com

DEBBIE MUMM
http://www.debbiemumm.com

FABRI-QUILT
http://www.fabri-quilt.com

RJR FASHION FABRICS
http://www.rjrfabrics.com

RJR offers a message board to help quilters locate fabric that they may have run out of and which is no longer manufactured.

FASCO FABRIC SALES COMPANY
http://www.clothworks-fabric.com

HOFFMAN CALIFORNIA FABRICS
http://www.hoffmanfabrics.com

THE HOFFMAN CHALLENGE
http://www.hoffmanchallenge.com

View this year's Hoffman Challenge fabric while learning about the challenge and how you can enter it. The site contains an exhibit schedule and pictures of past winning quilts.

IN THE BEGINNING FABRICS
http://www.inthebeginningfabrics.com

KINGS ROAD
http://www.kingsrd.com

KONA BAY
http://www.konabay.com

LUNN FABRICS
http://www.lunnfabrics.com

MARCUS BROTHERS TEXTILES INC.
http://www.marcusbrothers.com

P&B TEXTILES
http://www.pbtex.com

SOUTH SEA IMPORTS
http://www.southseaimports.com

WAVERLY FABRICS
http://www.decoratewaverly.com

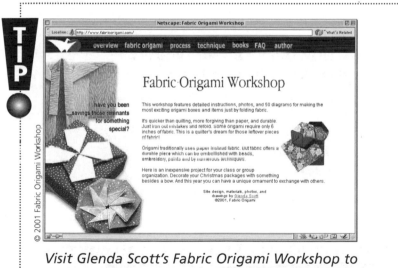

Visit Glenda Scott's Fabric Origami Workshop to Use Up All Those Scraps Glenda offers a cool site in which she shows how to take the concepts behind paper origami and apply them to fabric (**http://www.fabric origami.com**). Embellish your fabric origami with beads and embroidery.

Web Sites With Directories of Fabric Retailers, Both On the Web and Off

FABRIC COMPANY DIRECTORY FROM QUILTNET
http://quilt.com/FAQS/FabricCompaniesFaq.html

A list of fabric companies and their addresses compiled by members.

FABRICS.NET
http://www.fabrics.net

There are some really cool articles here on topics such as how to get custom fabric manufactured; fabric properties, plus a wonderful fabric question-and-answer column. Gridmar Publishing also offers info on where to buy fabrics and trim on the Web.

SEWING SEARCH
http://www.craftsearch.com/Sewing/index.html

You can locate fabric stores by zip code or name. You can also look up manufacturers.

THE COTTONWORKS FABRIC LIBRARY
http://www.cottoninc.com/FabricLibrary/ccl.cfm

A directory of over three hundred fabric makers with contact information.

THE ONLINE FABRIC DIRECTORY
http://www.inetcon.com/fabric

You can search for fabric stores by state—perfect if you're traveling.

SONJA KUEPPERS'S LIST OF PLACES TO BUY SILK
http://www.wam.umd.edu/~sek/wedding/silk.html

GLORIA'S TIPS FOR FABRIC "POWER SHOPPING" ON THE WEB

Face it, shopping for fabric on the Internet simply doesn't compare to shopping for it in person. You can't see it or feel it, and often scans of fabric on Web sites don't match the real thing in color or size of print. But if you're a fabriholic like Gloria, who's never seen a Hoffman or Kona Bay or RJR (the list goes on) fabric she didn't *have* to buy, you too will soon find yourself tapping your credit card into the Web sites of fabric stores. Here are Gloria's tips for fabric shopping by computer:

• Some fabric stores do a better job of scanning fabric to post on their Web sites than others do. Sometimes the fabric you get in the mail will look very different from what you saw on your computer screen. If you're buying fabric for a project where color and quality are critical, buy swatches first.

• Where should you look for fabric on the Web? Most of the big sewing Web sites (see Chapter 4) offer directories of links to Web sites of fabric stores that sell mail-order. We've listed some directories listed in this chapter.

• If you see a fabric that you like on the Web site of a fabric manufacturer, print the Web page, and jot down all the details about the fabric (like the name of the company, phone number, bolt number, etc.) and take it to your local fabric store. Some store owners may be willing to order it or track it down for you, although be warned that not all will do this. (Judy wanted to buy a special fabric from 3M Corp. that the company advertised on its Web site as available at a large national fabric store chain. She printed the Web page and took it to the store. The manager denied knowing anything about the fabric, and insisted the chain didn't carry it. She ended up visiting the store three more times with the copy of the Web page before the manager relented, called the national office, and tracked down the fabric for her.)

• Need yet another reason to splurge on fabric? Visit **15 Reasons to Buy Fabric (http://www5.palmnet.net/ ~smith/15reason.htm**) by the Beeline, Utah Quilt Guild. Among the compelling reasons given: It insulates the closet where it is kept and it is cheaper than psychiatric care.

Free Batting Advice and Information from Batting Manufacturers

Batting discussions on the Web can grow tense, especially when the all-cotton camp goes into combat with the cotton-poly blend camp. Our advice? Don't tell *anyone* the fiber content of the batting you use until you *really know* who your friends are.

**BATTING FAQ, FROM QUILTNET,
COURTESY OF SUE TRAUDT**
http://ttsw.com/FAQS/BattingFAQ.html

**BATTINGS, MIDDLE LAYER KEY
TO THE LOOK OF YOUR QUILT,
BY ADDY HARKAVY FOR PLANET PATCHWORK**
http://tvq.com/batting.htm

IDEAS FOR USING UP SCRAP FABRIC

Chances are you have a garbage bag full of fabric snips leftover from projects. You don't want to throw them out. Yet, you don't have enough of any particular fabric to piece anything except a crazy quilt. And some of the scraps are really ugly too. Here are Web sites with some rather ingenious patterns and ideas for using up scraps. Our favorite is the Scrappy Bargello found on Quiltville.

CRUMB PIECING
http://members.aol.com/crazyqltr1/crumb.htm

SCRAP QUILTS AND HOW TO MAKE THEM
http://members.aol.com/neadods/patch/patch.htm

STRING QUILTING
http://www.quiltville.com/stringx.html

THE INCREDIBLY SCRAPPY BARGELLO QUILT
http://www.quiltville.com/scrapbargello.html

"LOFTY DECISIONS, CHOOSING THE RIGHT BATTING, PART ONE—NATURAL FIBERS" BY LOIS VERMA

http://www.quiltersnewsletter.com/qnm/feature7.htm

PART TWO—SYNTHETIC FIBERS

http://www.quiltersnewsletter.com/qnm/feature8.htm

BUFFALO BATT AND FELT

http://www.superfluff.com

Makers of Buffalo Snow and Super Fluff.

FAIRFIELD: HOW TO CHOOSE A BATTING BY DONNA WILDER

http://www.poly-fil.com
http://www.poly-fil.com/crafts/HowToChooseBatting.html

HOBBS BINDED FIBERS

http://www.hobbsbondedfibers.com/Retail.htm

MOUNTAIN MIST

http://www.stearnstextiles.com/mountainmist

PERFECT COTTON

http://www.perfectcotton.com

QUILTER'S DREAM

http://www.quiltersdream.com

THE WARM COMPANY: WARM AND NATURAL BATTING FAQ

http://www.warmcompany.com
http://www.warmcompany.com/faq.html

ST. PETER'S WOOLEN MILL, INC.

http://www.woolenmill.com

Makers of Nature's Comfort wool batting.

JUDY'S TIPS FOR HUNTING FOR FABRIC IN WEB FLEA MARKETS

Judy's fabric obsessions are slightly different than Gloria's. She loves anything old and faded, and if it has cabbage roses or could be called "vintage," all the better. She loves fabric shopping on Web flea markets. Her favorite site is **eBay** (**http://www.ebay.com**). She uses the main searcher and searches for "fabric" or heads to the sewing goods category. This is a great place to hunt for old upholstery fabrics (the stuff someone had in their attic for decades, but never got around to using to reupholster that chair), as well as kitschy curtain fabrics from the '50s and '60s. Printed tea towels and tablecloths from the '50s can also be found in abundance. Judy's favorite find: 20 yards of hot pink pillow ticking from the '70s for $10—enough for a lifetime's worth of "retro" cat beds. Here are her tips for fabric flea marketing:

• If the fabric has a print find out how large it is.

• Find out what condition the fabric is in. Does it have any yellowing or fading? Any spots? How about signs of moths? And don't be afraid to ask what it smells like. Does it smell smoky or mildewy or reek of mothballs? Antique dealers in cyberspace are used to "smell" questions.

• Once you get the fabric, clean it thoroughly (put it through the washer twice) and keep it from your other fabric in case it has moths.

• Be sure to ask how much shipping will cost before you bid. The cost of shipping 20 yards of material might make it less of a bargain than you thought it was. See Chapter 1 for more Web flea marketing tips.

free Quilting Thread, Notions & Tools Advice

Where would we quilters be without our baskets full of quilting gadgets? The rotary cutters, marking pencils, glue sticks, rulers, and thimbles. It surprises us that some enterprising soul doesn't sell tool belts for quilters. Here's some of the advice on using and selecting quilting tools that you'll find on the Web. Need to know the best marking pencil, the right needle for the job? Searching for directions on how to build your own quilt frame? You'll find it all on some of these Web sites.

QUILTING TOOLS AND NOTIONS FROM THE WIDE WORLD QUILTING PAGE
http://ttsw.com/QuiltingTools.html

Sue Traudt offers a library of information on hoops, frames, notions, wall hangers, stencils, batting, and cutting and marking tools. Much of the advice has been compiled from conversations on the QuiltNet mailing list and the Usenet group rec.crafts.quilting.

NANCY ZIEMAN'S NANCY'S NOTIONS
http://www.nancysnotions.com

You'll find just about everything you need to know about any sewing tool at this marvelous Web site from Nancy of Sewing with Nancy fame. Head to the Sewing Library for lots of good articles.

CLOTILDE
http://www.clotilde.com

Tap into this site to request a free catalog of notions, another favorite among quilters.

THREADS MAGAZINE'S LIBRARY
http://www.taunton.com/th

Threads offers lots of fascinating articles from past issues on needles, thread and even quilt binding.

Free Needle & Thread Advice

"WHEN IS A NEEDLE MORE THAN A NEEDLE?" BY ROB HOLLAND
http://tvq.com/needles.htm

"WHAT YOU OUGHT TO KNOW ABOUT SEWING MACHINE NEEDLES" BY ROSE MARIE TONDL AT THE UNIVERSITY OF NEBRASKA
http://www.ianr.unl.edu/pubs/textiles/nf250.htm

SEW NEWS' MACHINE LIBRARY
http://www.sewnews.com/machines.htm

In this archive from Sew News you'll find tips, questions and answers, and articles such as "Thread Lubricant: Bon or Bane?"

CARYL FALLERT'S MACHINE QUILTING: THREAD QUESTIONS
http://www.bryerpatch.com/faq/machinequilting/mqthread.htm

THREAD TALES & TIPS BY SHEREE MCKEE
http://pages.prodigy.net/shereemckee/thread.htm

**T
I
P**

Free Thread Advice

Threads Magazine offers a great idea for making sewing machine needles easy to find in **Easy to Find Machine Needles** (**http://www.taunton.com/th/features/techniques/11easytofind.htm**). Take a marker and mark up a pincushion with special areas for each type of needle. There's a diagram to show you how.

SHAREE DAWN ROBERTS' THREAD TIPS
http://www.webofthread.com

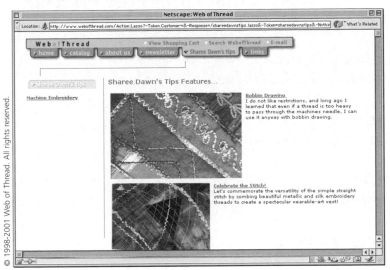

Select "Sharee Dawn's Tips" for advice on how to obtain spectacular results sewing with metallics and silk threads.

"THREAD FACTS" BY ROSE MARIE TONDL AND WENDY RICH AT THE UNIVERSITY OF NEBRASKA
http://www.ianr.unl.edu/pubs/textiles/nf37.htm

FRANCYNE'S THREAD 101
http://quilt.com/Bernina/Thread101.html

METALLIC THREADS AND THE SEWING MACHINE BY SHARLA HICKS
http://www.softexpressions.com/help/faq/faqmetallicthread.html

"UNCOMMON THREADS" BY LOIS MARILYN VERMA
http://www.quiltersnewsletter.com/qnm/feature18.htm

🛒 Web Homes of Thread and Ribbon Makers that Offer Free Projects and Advice

COATS & CLARK
http://www.coatsandclark.com

DMC
http://www.dmc-usa.com

GLITZ
http://www.glitz.com

GUTERMANN
http://www.guetermann.com

KREINIK MANUFACTURING COMPANY, INC.
http://www.kreinik.com

MADEIRA THREAD
http://www.madeirathreads.com

OFFRAY RIBBON
http://www.offray.com/prod.html

SULKY OF AMERICA
http://www.sulky.com

SUPERIOR THREADS
http://www.superiorthreads.com

YLI
http://www.ylicorp.com

Free Advice on Quilting Hoops and Frames

QUILTING FRAMES AND HOOPS FROM THE WORLD WIDE QUILTING PAGE
http://ttsw.com/Tools/HoopsAndFrames.html

Sue Traudt provides a compilation of addresses of quilt frame and hoop makers, and advice that has been posted as messages in the QuiltNet mailing list, the newsgroup rec.crafts.quilting, and the America Online quilting forum.

FLOOR FRAME INSTRUCTIONS BY KATHY SOMERS
http://www.quiltchat.com/lessons/floorframe.html

"HOW TO MAKE A QUILT HOOP STAND" BY SUSAN M.
http://www.quilt.com/miscquilting/hoopstanddirections.html

"BEYOND THE LAP HOOP" BY ADDY HARKAVY
http://tvq.com/frames.htm

HOW TO ATTACH A QUILT TO YOUR THREE-POLE FRAME FROM HINTERBERG DESIGN, INC.
http://www.hinterberg.com
http://www.hinterberg.com/attach.htm

QUILT FRAME ADVICE FROM GRACE FRAME
http://www.graceframe.com/graceq&a.htm

QUESTIONS TO ASK WHEN BUYING A FLOOR FRAME
http://www.jasmineheirlooms.com/buyingafloorframequestions.htm

QUESTIONS TO ASK WHEN BUYING A HOOP STAND
http://www.jasmineheirlooms.com/buyingahoopstand questions.htm

FLYNN MULTI FRAME TIPS
http://www.flynnquilt.com/quiltingtips.html

Free Advice on Other Sewing Notions

EZ INTERNATIONAL TOOL TUTORIAL
http://www.ezquilt.com

Select "Tutorials" from the left menu to learn how to cut hexagons, equilateral triangles, triangles, and diamonds at this well-illustrated site.

FISKARS SCISSORS
http://www.fiskars.com

At the Web site of this scissors maker you'll find free craft products and snipping advice.

ROWENTA IRONS
http://www.rowentausa.com/irons/irons.htm

Learn about all the options available in the Cadillac of irons, and how to use and care for them.

KWIK SQUARES—THE TRIANGLE SQUARE CALCULATOR DEMO PAGE
http://www.mwaz.com/quilt/calculat.htm

Kwik Squares offers a nifty explanation of making quick-pieced triangle units from squares.

MARKING PENCIL INFORMATION
http://www.prairienet.org/community/clubs/quilts/pencils.html

Read some casual test results of using various fabric marking pencils.

OLFA
http://www.olfa.com/home.asp

*Be sure to visit Olfa Safety (**http://www.olfa.com/safety.asp**) for general safety considerations.*

 # Free Advice on Stencils

THE STENCIL COMPANY
http://quiltingstencils.com/index.html

The Stencil Company answers quilt design questions, many having to do with stencils, on topics like quilting concentric circles, set-in piecing techniques, and quilting Celtic patterns.

AMERICAN TRADITIONAL STENCILS
http://www.Amtrad-stencil.com

Want to learn how to use stencils to emboss? This site includes a marvelous projects page.

STENSOURCE INTERNATIONAL
http://www.stensource.com

StenSource offers many home decorating stencils, but you'll also find plenty of quilting stencil designs, a glossary of stenciling terms, and answers to frequently asked questions.

free Quilt Embellishment How-Tos

B e honest: you don't *really* want someone to sit on your quilt, do you? You want to be-ribbon it, be-bow it, bead it, embroider it, and festoon it with lace, buttons, charms, rick-rack, and all manner of gewgaws. There are many Web sites dedicated to helping you achieve embellishment excess on your quilts, so many that we've decided to devote an entire chapter to them.

Web Crazy Quilting Mania!

They're everywhere on the Web, spreading their enthusiasm for quilts without any plan or orderly design. That's not surprising since the Web is itself a crazy quilt of jagged intentions and kaleidoscopic colors. Who better to populate it than crazy quilters?

THE CRAZY QUILT MAILING LIST
http://www.quiltropolis.com

Conceived by Dawn Smith and run by Beth Ober of Quiltropolis, this bubbly group of crazy quilt fans discusses hand and machine embroidery on quilts; lace, bead, button, and ribbon embellishment; books and classes on crazy quilts; and more. To sign up head to Quiltropolis.

THE CRAZY QUILT SOCIETY
http://www.crazyquilt.com

The Crazy Quilt Society is a program of the Quilt Heritage Foundation. Membership is $25 per year. Benefits include a newsletter and annual conferences. Esteemed members include Judith Baker Montano, Penny McMorris, Leslie Levison, and Cindy Brick (newsletter editor).

Web Sites with Fabric Embellishment Advice

FABRIC EMBELLISHMENT FROM ABOUT.COM
http://sewing.about.com/hobbies/sewing/library/weekly/
aa052298.htm

*Debbie Colgrove, who hosts the sewing forum at About.Com
(http://sewing.about.com), offers ongoing articles on fabric
embellishment.*

DYED & GONE TO HEAVEN BY CARON
http://caron-net.com

*Thread-maker Caron hosts a wonderful Web site filled with
"online classes" that explore different embellishment techniques
with Caron threads.*

PURRFECTION ARTISTIC WEARABLES' PERFECTLY FREE PROJECTS
http://www.purrfection.com
http://www.purrfection.com/projects/index.htm

*Head to the Project link where you'll find directions for discharge
dyeing with Comet Liquid Gel, embossing velvet, inlay weaving,
making popcorn fabric, and other fabric embellishment techniques perfect for jazzing up your quilts.*

MAKING GREAT SLASH FABRICS
http://www.make-it-easy.com/slastec2.html

*Nancy L. Restuccia explains how to do this centuries-old tech-
nique, currently called "Faux Chenille."*

Bargain Buttons

Ebay (**http://www.ebay.com**) is a great place to hunt for
beads and other embellishments, such as antique buttons, ribbons, and lace. Use the service's main searcher
to hunt for words like "Czech beads" or "buttons." (Be
sure to read our tips in Chapter 1 for bargain hunting in
Web flea markets.)

▦ Web Sites with Advice on Embroidery and Ribbon Embellishment

WONDERFUL STITCHES WWW
http://www.needlework.com

You'll find lots of information on cross-stitch, quilting, needle-point, and other decorative forms of stitching.

KATHLEEN DYER'S COUNTED CROSS-STITCH, NEEDLEWORK, AND STITCHERY PAGE
http://www.dnai.com/~kdyer

This is a fantastic Web site with links to embroidery information all over the Internet, plus free tutorials and charts.

SHARON BOGGON'S NEEDLEWORK STITCH DICTIONARY
http://www.anu.edu.au/ITA/CSA/textiles/sharonb/stitches/stitchfsite.html

Sharon, in Canberra, Australia, offers a large and beautifully illustrated Web-based embroidery stitch dictionary in which you can look up tutorials for specific stitches. She asks that users mail her something from their scrap bag as "shareware payment."

Read the Sad Tale of the Nancy Drew Quilt
Judy has always been a big fan of Nancy Drew novels. So she decided to make a quilt by transferring art from the books onto fabric with her ink-jet printer. Little did she know what a fuss Simon & Schuster's attorneys would raise. Read the full story, see the partially censored quilt, and find out what precautions you should take before you put other peoples' art in your quilt (**http://www.execpc.com/~judyheim/qcc2.html**).

THE EMBROIDERY MALL
http://wwww.EmbroideryMall.com

*You'll find information on supplies, free designs, lots of articles on embroidery, and an embroidery discussion group. Take a look at the Embroidery Mall's library (**http://www.embroiderymall .com/library/**) for a thread database and much more.*

THE NEEDLEARTS MALL
http://www.needlearts.com/shop_index.html

Although this is a commercial site, with links to embroidery-related retailers, it's nearly a magazine with articles on different aspects of stitching, tutorials, lessons, and much more.

THE CHARTED DESIGNERS OF AMERICA RIBBON EMBROIDERY PAGE
http://www.stitching.com/CDA/ribbon.htm

You'll find lots of instructions and illustrations on perfecting your ribbon embroidery stitches.

HOW TO MAKE DIMENSIONAL OR RUCHED FLOWERS, FROM SUE TRAUDT'S WORLD WIDE QUILTING WEB SITE
http://ttsw.com/Bernina/Challenge96/Lesson5.html

Web Sites with Advice on Beading

BEAD NET
http://www.mcs.net/~simone/beadnet.html

Bead Net, by Simone Oettinger, offers an incredible library of information on beading including advice on selecting and using beads, links to other beading sites and manufacturers' Web sites (like a company that offers "beaded appliqués"), plus a "cyber-bead embroiders" page.

BEADWORK AT ABOUT.COM
http://beadwork.about.com

Paula S. Morgan is your guide to the world of beading on the Web. There are lots of articles on beads and techniques, plus links to the Web sites of beading fans.

THE BEADWRANGLER'S BEAD & FIBER JUNCTION
http://www.beadwrangler.com

The Beadwrangler offers over a thousand pages of beading information. Be sure to visit Tips & Techniques (http://www.beadwrangler.com/tips&techniques.htm) for inspiring ways to incorporate beading into your work.

THE BEAD FAIRIES PAGE
http://members.home.net/sdsantan/beadfairies.html

This site offers lots of tips, tutorials, patterns, and resources and links to other beading Web sites, including bead shops on the Web.

free Fabric Dyeing & Painting How-Tos

Sure, billions of bolts of fabric cram the stores, but there are times when you *still* can't find what you want. If you've ever had a hankering to create your own fabric designs, either through dyeing or painting, there's a Web site out there to help you. As usual, other quilters who've been-there-done-that are your best source of information. Here's how to find them, their advice, and their Web pages.

Free Discussion Groups for Quilters Interested in Dyeing

DYERS E-MAIL LIST
http://www.art.emich.edu/lists/dyerslist/dyerslist.html

Pat Williams of the art department of Eastern Michigan University hosts this wonderful group, which discusses immersion dyeing and the application of synthetic dyes, textile pigments, and other chemicals on fabric. You can read past messages that have been posted to Dyers at:
http://www.art.emich.edu/lists/dyerslist/search.html

YAHOO! SILK PAINTING CLUB
http://clubs.yahoo.com/clubs/silkpainting

Tap in to chat with others about techniques, suppliers, and experiences in silk painting.

 ### NATURAL DYES MAILING LIST & ARCHIVES
http://www47.pair.com/lindo/dyelist.htm

Mara Riley's list is for those interested in using plants and "gentle" homemade dyes.

Free Dyeing Recipes and Advice

DYEING RECIPES AND ADVICE
FROM *RUG HOOKING MAGAZINE*
http://www.rughookingonline.com

Rug Hooking Magazine offers terrific articles and recipes from their archives that will have you dyeing wool with onion skins, dyeing in an electric fry pan, and performing the art of "salt shaker dyeing." Some include:

• ADVENTURES IN DYEING: EXPERIENCED DYERS SHARE THEIR TECHNIQUES
http://www.rughookingonline.com/dyeing/adventures.html

• HANGING AROUND WAITING TO DYE: THE SECRETS OF COAT HANGER DYEING"
BY JANE MCGOWN FLYNN
http://www.rughookingonline.com/waiting/hanger.html

• BASIC JAR DYEING INSTRUCTIONS
BY MARYANNE LINCOLN
http://www.rughookingonline.com/basic/jardye.html

• RECIPES FROM THE DYE KITCHEN
BY MARYANNE LINCOLN
http://www.rughookingonline.com/archives.html

PAULA BURCH'S ALL ABOUT HAND DYEING FABRIC
http://www.flash.net/~pburch/dyeing.html

QUILTNET DYEING ADVICE

Sue Traudt's World Wide Quilting offers several collections of messages that members of the quilting E-mail discussion group QuiltNet have written over the years. These are excellent sources of advice:

- **QUILTNET ON TEA-DYING**
  http://quilt.com/FAQS/TeaDyingFAQ.html

- **QUILTNET ON HAND DYEING FABRIC**
  http://quilt.com/FAQS/FabricDyingFAQ.html

- **QUILTNET ON DISCHARGE DYEING**
  http://quilt.com/FAQS/DischargeDyeingFAQ.html

- **QUILTNET ON FABRIC DYE SAFETY**
  http://quilt.com/FAQS/DyeSafetyFaq.html

- **QUILTNET ON IMAGE TRANSFERS, FABRIC DYEING, AND PAINTING**
  http://ttsw.com/HowTo/FabricImaging.html

DYEING FABRIC BY CYNTHIA BONNER
http://www.nmia.com/~mgdesign/qor/technique/dyeing.htm

T I P

Don't Dye It, Buy It!

Lots of quilters on the Internet sell hand-dyed fabric. Just sign on to any of the dyeing mailing lists and ask.

T I P

Want to Learn How to Silkscreen?

Tap into *Screenprinting 101—A Beginner's Guide* (**http://www.printlee.com/scprint101/screenprinting_101.htm**), courtesy of **The Press**. An illustrated step-by-step lesson plan walks you through the process from stretching a frame to the final cure. Learn how to stop-clean a misprint and the procedure for proper clean-up.

~~FABRIC DYEING WITH KOOL-AID~~
BY DAWN DUPERAULT
http://www.reddawn.net/quilt/koolaid.htm

You read it on the Web first! Exciting new colors can be as close as your kid's cup of Kool-Aid.

THE WOAD PAGE
http://www.net-link.net/~rowan/crafts/woad/woadpage.html

This lively Web site, by "Rowan" of the Society for Creative Anachronism, is devoted to the study and use of woad, a blue dye plant used to dye fabrics—and paint bodies since medieval times.

"BASIC INSTRUCTIONS FOR WORKING WITH REACTIVE AND WASHFAST ACID DYES" BY PAT WILLIAMS OF EASTERN MICHIGAN UNIVERSITY
http://www.art.acad.emich.edu/faculty/williams/basicdyeinstr.html

🛒 CARYL FALLERT'S
FABRIC DYEING AND PAINTING FAQ
http://www.bryerpatch.com/faq/dyeing.htm

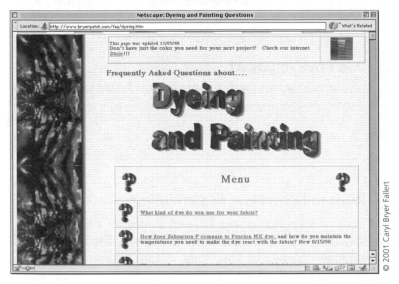

Quilt-artist Fallert answers questions such as "What kind of dye do you use for your fabric?" and "How does Sabracron F compare to Procion MX dye?"

"INSTRUCTIONS FOR SPECIAL WAYS OF WORKING WITH DYES AND RELATED CHEMICALS" BY PAT WILLIAMS

http://www.art.acad.emich.edu/faculty/williams/specialdye
 instr.html

🛒 STUDIO SAFETY AND GUIDELINES FROM PRO CHEMICAL & DYE

http://www.prochemical.com/store/studio.htm

"A SIMPLE METHOD OF ONE-POT, MULTI-COLOR DYEING" BY SUSAN DRUDING AND SUSIE HODGES

http://www.straw.com/sig/multipot.html

Dye experts Susan Druding and Susie Hodges reveal a straight-forward recipe for dyeing protein fibers like wool, silk, and nylon with acid wool dyes.

HOW TO TEA DYE BY DAWN DUPERAULT

http://www.reddawn.net/quilt/teadye.htm

Dawn explains how to achieve an older, antique look to your fabrics by using tea bags.

"SPACE-DYEING IN A CROCK-POT" BY GLENNA STANSIFER

http://members.aol.com/FiberNews/glenna.html

In this intriguing article from Fiber News, Glenna describes how she dyes twisted strands of fiber or fabric in a Crock-Pot using unsweetened Kool-Aid or Easter-egg dye, and mayonnaise jars. By "space-dyeing" she refers to dyeing the fabric so that bands of colors run along it.

"NATURAL DYEING WITH OXALIS FLOWERS ON COTTON" BY JANIS SAUNDER

http://members.aol.com/FiberNews/janis.html

FOAM DYEING FROM SUSAN NORTH

http://www.redmoonquilts.com/page26.html

Mixing shaving cream with dye can create some interesting effects.

"SURFACE APPLICATION RECIPES FOR PROCION OR OTHER FIBER REACTIVE DYES" BY SUSAN DRUDING

http://www.straw.com/sig/procion.html

DYE IT BLACK FAQ

http://www.cclabs.missouri.edu/~c510292/gothic/dye.faq.html

A few years ago "gothic" or all-black attire was popular with the hip set. Directions for dyeing everything in one's closet black were pandemic on the Internet. "Lady Bathory," a dye-shop technician at the University of Tennessee, Knoxville theatre costume shop reveals how to dye just about everything imaginable, including velvets, to the blackest black possible.

GRADUATED FABRIC DYEING

http://www.quiltchat.com/lessons/dying.html

Kathy Somers explains graduated fabric dyeing with Procion fiber-reactive dyes.

POTATO DEXTRIN RESIST FROM SUSAN NORTH

http://www.redmoonquilts.com/page27.html

Learn about the interesting effects you can achieve with potato dextrin resist and dye or bleach.

DISCHARGE DYEING WITH COMET LIQUID GEL

http://www.purrfection.com/projects/dischargedye.htm

The folks at Purrfection Artistic Wearables explain how to use liquid Comet to create unique fabric.

"METHODS OF DISCHARGING DYE" BY PAT WILLIAMS

http://www.art.acad.emich.edu/faculty/williams/specialdyeinstr
.html#discharge

Pat explains methods of removing color from previously dyed textiles.

DYEING FABRIC IN THE MICROWAVE
FROM THE COTTON CLUB
http://www.cottonclub.com/dying.htm

PAINT AND DYEING AT THE UNIVERSITY OF
ALASKA, FAIRBANKS THEATRICAL COSTUME SHOP
http://costumes.org/pages/dyeing.htm

Find out how UAF costumers painted tuxedos with leopard patterns for the prom scene in Grease *and outfited the entire cast of* Comedy of Errors *without sewing a stitch—they painted all the costumes.*

DYEING WITH BLEACH
BY LOIS ERICSON AND THREADS
http://www.taunton.com/th/features/fitandfabric/bleach/1.htm

Lois details how you can make extraordinary patterns on dark fabric with ordinary household bleach.

Free Marbling How-tos

QUILTNET ON FABRIC MARBLING
http://quilt.com/FAQS/MarbledFabricFAQ.html

Quilters in the QuiltNet discussion group exchange tips for marbling fabric, a compilation courtesy of the World Wide Quilting page.

FAQS ABOUT MARBLING
FROM LINDA MORAN OF MARBLE-T DESIGN, L.L.C.
http://www.marbledfab.com/faqs.html

A GLIMPSE INTO MARJORIE BEVIS'
MARBLING PROCESS
http://www.marbledfabrics.com/aglimpse.htm

A BRIEF HISTORY OF MARBLING BY MARJORIE BEVIS
http://www.marbledfabrics.com/history.htm

"HAND MARBLING FOR QUILTERS"
BY JANET WICKELL
http://www.scrapquilts.com/marble.html

Janet offers a complete illustrated tutorial on the marbling process, including resources.

Free Silk Painting, Shibori, and Batik Advice

BATIK IN INDONESIA
http://www.expat.or.id/info/batik.html

You'll read a fascinating history of batik, Indonesia's favorite art form. You can see the step-by-step process of the making of a batik (http://www.expat.or.id/info/batiksteps.html).

SILK PAINTING GALLERY
http://www.silkpaintinggallery.com

Francine Dufour explains the basics of painting on silk. Her painting tips include advice on setting colors in silk, what a giclee is, and a basic supply list. There is a silk gallery, events, and related resources.

THE BASICS OF SILK PAINTING
http://www.sassisilks.com/silkpainting.html

This is a great site with introductory material on different types of silk painting.

THE UK GUILD OF SILK PAINTERS
http://www.silkpainters-guild.co.uk/index2.html

Membership is open to all.

"MAKING SHIBORI FABRIC" BY COZY BENDESKY
http://www.erols.com/cozy/shibori1.html

 SHIBORI TECHNIQUE
http://www.slip.net/~redtail/ninshibar/technique.htm

🛒 SHI-BO-RI JAPAN MUSEUM
http://www.shibori.co.jp

*Visit this amazing cyber-museum to understand more of the traditional art of Japanese tie-dyeing known as shibori. Be sure to visit **Shi-Bo-Ri Techniques** (**http://www.shibori.co.jp/tec/index.html**) for a discussion on traditional techniques, patterns, tying methods, and more.*

INTRODUCTION TO BATIK
http://www.goodorient.com/intobat.html

After reading the introduction, follow the links for articles on preparing and making batik, and view a selection of batik clothing. From the Good Orient Company of Singapore.

BATIK TUTORIAL FROM CRAFTOWN
http://www.craftown.com/batik.htm

Craftown explains how to use wax and dye to create beautiful fabric.

HOW TO DO HOT-WAX BATIK USING DYLON DYES
http://www.textiles.org.nz/dylon/batikhowto.htm

🛒 Web Sites of Fabric Paint and Dye Suppliers

DHARMA TRADING COMPANY
http://www.dharmatrading.com/index.html

You'll find lots of instructions on topics like stream-setting silk dyes, dye painting, discharge paste instructions, tie-dyeing silk in the microwave, and more.

PRO CHEMICAL & DYE, INC.
http://www.prochemical.com
http://www.prochemical.com/store/dirindex.htm

You'll find answers to questions on MX reactive dyes such as "Why can't I get a gray by using less black dye powder?" There are also instructions on how to obtain the popular suede look when dyeing, creating starburst patterns on silk and cotton, do graduation dyeing, and more.

DECO ARTS
http://www.decoart.com

Deco Arts, maker of textiles paints, offers advice and project directions.

JACQUARD PRODUCTS
http://www.jacquardproducts.com
http://www.jacquardproducts.com/productpages/technical/
technique.htm

Gloria highly recommends Jacquard fabric paint. The site includes paint and dyeing tips on topics like chemical resist dyeing methods, print paste recipes, scrunch dyeing, and stamping velvet.

G&S DYE
http://www.gsdye.com/index.html
http://www.gsdye.com/Canada/instructional_sheets.html

G&S offers a wide range of information and instruction sheets. Topics include Procion MX dyes, Procion H dyes, acid dyes, screen printing, and marbling. Techniques include immersion dyeing, direct application tie-dye, batik using MX dyes, microwave scarf painting, and sun printing.

MENDEL'S
http://www.mendels.com
http://www.mendels.com/tiedye.html

Mendel's is an art supply and fabric store in San Francisco's Haight-Ashbury. What better place to go for directions and supplies for tie-dyeing?

EARTH GUILD
http://www.earthguild.com
http://www.earthguild.com/products/Riffs/riffs.htm

You'll find instructions for Procion immersion dyeing, tie-dyeing, batik, marbling, dyeing with indigo, and natural dyeing.

Dye Your Own Threads

Quilting with overdyed cottons is very popular. In "Dyeing Needlepoint Threads" (**http://needlepoint. about.com/hobbies/needlepoint/library/weekly/aa062698 .htm**) Janet Perry explains how to dye threads with Kool-Aid, Jell-O, tea, and other kitchen supplies.

free Help for Transferring Photos to Fabric

What quilter doesn't dream of making a memory quilt someday? You know, one of those evocative quilts designed around fabric reproductions of favorite family photos. There are a number of ways to get a photo onto fabric. You can scan the photo into your computer, then print it directly on pre-treated fabric with your computer's printer. You can print the photo on special paper that you iron onto your fabric. Or, you can copy the photo onto special paper with a color copier, then iron it onto fabric.

But whatever method you choose, you need to follow the steps carefully or else the photo won't be colorfast, and will run in the wash. (In fact, nearly every week we receive E-mail from quilters who've printed photos onto muslin and want to know how to make the image colorfast. We have to break it to them that the fabric needs to be specially pre-treated before they print the photo on the fabric or else there's no way to make the image permanent.) The Web sites in this chapter will fill you in on the different methods for getting a photo onto fabric, and keeping it there. We recommend reading all their advice before you plunge off and start printing photos onto your quilt fabric.

QUILTNET ON IMAGE TRANSFERS, FABRIC DYEING, AND PAINTING
http://ttsw.com/HowTo/FabricImaging.html

Sue Traudt's World Wide Quilting Web site maintains this collection of messages culled from the discussion group QuiltNet on transferring photos to fabric.

PRINTING ON FABRIC BY BETTY SZYMANSKI
http://www.compuquilt.com/prtonfab.htm

TRANSFER PRINTING ON FABRICS WITH COMPUTER OR COLOR COPIER, PART 1 AND PART 2, BY SUSAN C. DRUDING

http://quilting.about.com/hobbies/quilting/library/weekly/aa061999.htm

http://quilting.about.com/hobbies/quilting/library/bl_aa061999.htm

Susan explains the various methods for printing on fabric, including using a computer ink-jet printer and color copiers, and sublimation.

BUBBLE JET SET INFORMATION PAGE FROM CARYL FALLERT

http://www.bryerpatch.com/faq/bjs.htm

Master quiltmaker Caryl Fallert explains how to use this product and offers tips for soaking, washing, ironing, and printing your fabric.

PLAYING WITH PHOTOS

http://www.quiltersnewsletter.com/qnm/feature14.htm

This article, originally from Quilt It For Kids and presented by Quilter's Newsletter Magazine, discusses several methods of transferring photos to fabric.

DIRECT PRINTING ON FABRIC WITH A COMPUTER BY SUSAN C. DRUDING

http://quilting.about.com/hobbies/quilting/library/weekly/aa101100.htm

This article focuses on Bubble Jet Set, a product designed to make ink-jet ink permanent. Resources are included.

🛒 HANES T-SHIRTS

http://www.hanes2u.com

Hanes offers loads of tips, tutorials, and projects for creating iron-on fabric transfers with ink-jet printers. You can use them to make quilts.

free Advice on Appraising, Cleaning & Storing Quilts

Who doesn't want to display their beautiful quilts for all the world to see? But where and how you display them can mean all the difference in how well they hold up over time. Sunlight is your quilt's worst enemy, but there are others like sweaty hands and stains. Many Web sites offer free advice on repairing, cleaning, and storing quilts. Some sites also offer advice on obtaining appraisals of quilts for insurance. Our favorite sites are the stain removal ones where you specify a stain and the site tells you how to remove it.

Free Quilt Display, Storage, Cleaning & Conservation Advice

CONSERVATION/PRESERVATION INFORMATION FOR THE GENERAL PUBLIC
http://palimpsest.stanford.edu/bytopic/genpub

Stanford University maintains this mega-site of information on conservation.

THE CARE AND PRESERVATION OF ANTIQUE TEXTILES AND COSTUMES
http://www.hfmgv.org/histories/cis/textile.html

A product of The Henry Ford Museum and Greenfield Village, this Web site explains how to minimize or eliminate things that can damage antique textiles and offers basic advice on handling, displaying, storing, and cleaning.

PRESERVING YOUR ANTIQUE QUILT FROM *THE ANTIQUES ROADSHOW*
http://www.pbs.org/wgbh/pages/roadshow/tips/quilts.html

QUILT CARE ARTICLES
FROM LOST QUILT COME HOME
http://www.lostquilt.com/QuiltCare.html

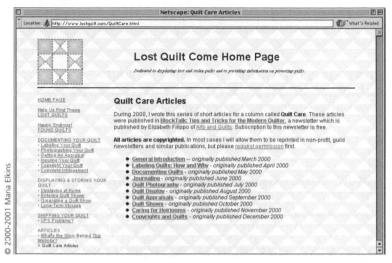

Articles include how and why to label a quilt, documenting, display, caring for heirlooms, and other care topics.

THE AMERICAN INSTITUTE FOR CONSERVATION OF HISTORIC AND ARTISTIC WORKS
http://aic.stanford.edu

"Caring For Textiles" (**http://aic.stanford.edu/treasure/ textiles.html**) and *"Salvaging Water Damaged Textiles"* (**http://aic.stanford.edu/disaster/txsalv.html**) *are two valuable articles offered at this great site.*

"STORING WEDDING GOWNS AND TEXTILE HEIRLOOMS" BY JOYCE A. SMITH AND NORMA PITTS AT OHIO STATE
http://www.ag.ohio-state.edu/~ohioline/hyg-fact/5000/5545.html

PRESERVING QUILTS IN YOUR HOME
FROM THE MUSEUM OF FLORIDA HISTORY
http://www.dos.state.fl.us/dhr/museum/acs_1.html

CLEANING ANTIQUE QUILTS
http://www.quilthistory.com/cleaning.htm

"HOW DO I STORE ANTIQUE TEXTILES AT HOME?" BY THE SMITHSONIAN
http://www.si.edu/resource/faq/nmah/antqtext.htm

The Smithsonian offers free advice on storing a variety of antique textiles at home, including quilts, but also tapestries, rugs, and costumes.

"CARE OF VICTORIAN SILK QUILTS AND SLUMBER THROWS," BY THE SMITHSONIAN
http://www.si.edu/resource/faq/nmah/vicquilt.htm

Learn the best way to care for lavishly stitched Victorian needlework, including how to repair, clean, and store it.

"QUICK, DAMAGE-FREE QUILT HANGING" FROM *THREADS MAGAZINE*
http://www.taunton.com/th/features/techniques/28quiltclip.htm

MOUNTS FOR OVERSIZED FLAT TEXTILES: PAPER HONEYCOMB VS. HDPE BY ELIZABETH M. RED ELK
http://palimpsest.stanford.edu/waac/wn/wn14/wn14-3/
 wn14-309.html

THE ROCKY MOUNTAIN QUILT MUSEUM QUILT PRESERVATION ADVICE
http://www.rmqm.org/preservi.htm

ILLINI COUNTRY STITCHERS' TEXTILE PRESERVATION RESOURCES (ESPECIALLY FOR QUILTERS)
http://www.prairienet.org/community/clubs/quilts
http://www.prairienet.org/community/clubs/quilts/Preserve/
 pres.html

The Champaign, Illinois quilt guild offers a list of Web sites devoted to textile preservation, and also a bibliography of good books on preservation, many published by museums.

"ON WASHING QUILTS" BY ADDY HARKAVY
http://planetpatchwork.com/wash.htm

CARING FOR YOUR QUILT
http://www.stearnstextiles.com/mountainmist/tutor/tutor2.htm

Learn how to wash a quilt and why dry-cleaning is not recommended. You'll find hand-washing as well as machine-washing advice.

CONSERVATION HANDOUTS
FROM THE BISHOP MUSEUM IN HAWAII
http://www.bishop.hawaii.org/bishop/conservation/
conservation.html

Bishop Museum publishes a variety of pamphlets on conservation, and many are available for reading on its Web site. Among them: "Bugs Are Eating My Family Treasures," "Wet Cleaning Quilts at Home," "Care of Feathers," "Archival Mounts For Paintings on Textiles," "Bleaching," and "Caring for Tapa." The museum also offers books on conservation that one can order.

"THE DISPLAY AND CARE OF ART QUILTS"
BY APRIL NIINO, PENNY NII QUILT ART
http://206.204.3.133/dir_nii/nii_dat_quicar.html

The Penny Nii gallery offers advice on hanging, storing, and cleaning quilts, as well as combating the effects of sunlight.

THE CARE AND FEEDING OF ANTIQUE QUILTS
BY DAWN DUPERAULT
http://www.reddawn.net/quilt/antique.htm

"CARING FOR ANTIQUE QUILTS"
BY BARB VAN VIERZEN
http://www.kawartha.net/~jleonard/quilts.htm

From the Peterborough Centennial Museum and Archives comes advice on storing, airing, and cleaning old quilts (and photographs).

WORLD WIDE QUILTING'S QUILT CARE ADVICE
http://ttsw.com/HowTo/QuiltCare.html

Sue Traudt's World Wide Quilting Web site offers a collection of ideas and comments on quilt care gathered from members of the QuiltNet mailing list discussion group, AOL Quilters Online, and Usenet. Subjects include washing quilts and handling faded fabrics.

CARYL FALLERT'S SHIPPING, HANGING AND STORAGE TIPS
http://www.bryerpatch.com/faq/storage.htm

© Caryl Fallert

QUILT AND TEXTILE STORAGE FROM DAWN DUPERAULT
http://www.reddawn.net/quilt/storage.htm

"CONSERVATION OF TEXTILE ITEMS" BY SHIRLEY NIEMEYER AND PATRICIA COX CREWS
http://www.ianr.unl.edu/pubs/textiles/nf137.htm

The University of Nebraska Extension article offers advice on cleaning, care, storage, and display of treasured textiles.

THE KIRK COLLECTION
http://www.kirkcollection.com

You'll find lots of information on quilt care and conservation on this Web site of The Kirk Collection in Omaha, Nebraska. Kirk specializes in mail-order sales of reproduction fabrics, conservation products like acid-free tissue and storage boxes, and books on quilt restoration and conservation. The company also sponsors a Quilt Restoration Society and conferences.

"HOW I WASH MY QUILTS" BY JOANNA BARNES
http://wso.williams.edu/~jbarnes/quilting/wash.htm

THE QUILTBROKER
http://www.quiltbroker.com/quilt_storage.html

Should you wrap your quilts in buffered or unbuffered acid-free tissue? Should you store your quilts on tubes? The QuiltBroker answers such questions and many more on its quilt storage information page. The company also sells acid-free tissue and boxes and care labels.

 # Free Appraisal Advice

ARE YOU CONSIDERING AN INTERNET APPRAISAL FOR YOUR QUILTED TEXTILE?
http://www.quiltappraisers.org/internetappraisal.html

PROFESSIONAL ASSOCIATION OF APPRAISERS QUILTED TEXTILES
http://www.quiltappraisers.org

All members of the PAAQT are certified by the American Quilters Society. A list of certified appraisers and contact information are included.

DEBORAH ROBERTS' QUILT APPRAISAL PAGE
http://quilt.com/DebbieRoberts/appraise.htm

Certified quilt appraiser Roberts explains why you should get your quilts appraised and how to hire an appraiser. Her site includes a list of appraisers certified by the American Quilter's Society and who can be E-mailed. These appraisers are qualified to appraise fair market, insurance, and donation values of quilts. Roberts also provides quilt care, labeling, and storage advice.

APPRAISING YOUR QUILTS, PART 1
http://www.shellyquilts.com/Appraisingquilt1.html

APPRAISING YOUR QUILTS, PART II
http://www.shellyquilts.com/Appraisingquilt2.html

Shelly Zegart explains the common types of appraisals, how you find an appraiser, the elements of a correctly prepared appraisal, and more.

 # Free Stain Removal Help

It's happened to all of us. Your significant other slops spaghetti sauce on your great-grandma's quilt, or a guest plops a taco casserole on your painstakingly hand-pieced table runner. Quick! Before the stain sets, tap into one of these Web sites for directions on stain exorcism. You can also head to any of the major Web searchers like **Excite!** (**http://www.excite.com**) and type in, say, "ketchup stain" to find Web sites with removal directions. But in all honesty, we still prefer Heloise's well-tested stain removal tips!

THE RESOURCE: TEXTILES, CLOTHING & DESIGN
http://www.ianr.unl.edu/pubs/Textiles

The University of Nebraska Cooperative Extension offers advice on handling the sorts of stains and odors that often infect rural quilts: skunk perfume, pesticide stench, smoke odors, and mildew. The site even offers advice on how to salvage textiles from floods. The university offers online versions of many of its other publications on textile care.

THE TIDE CLOTHESLINE
http://www.clothesline.com

Calling itself "the most comprehensive site on the Web dedicated to keeping your clothes looking their best," detergent-maker Tide offers an interactive Stain Detective to help you rub out spots. Select your spot maker from a list of hundreds, choose the fabric type and specify whether it's white or printed. The Stain Detective will come up with a remedy (although washing in Tide is always the last step). Some of the directions advise to merely use "stain remover" but some are pretty clever.

Fabric care tips, garment labeling advice, and tips for keeping children's clothes clean are also available. Be careful, though: after visiting this site you may suffer the urge to run to the washing machine and spend the day laundering.

FABRICLINK
http://www.fabriclink.com

Kathy and Tom Swantko created and maintain this huge resource of unbiased educational information on fabric. **Fiber University (http://www. fabriclink.com/University.html)** *offers a fiber history, characteristics of textile fibers, fabric care 101, a dictionary of fabric terms, flammability and safety issues, and more. This is a must-bookmark site!*

WORLD WIDE QUILTING'S STAIN REMOVAL FAQ
http://quilt.com/FAQS/StainRemovalFAQ.html

Sue Traudt has compiled all the stain removal advice proffered in the QuiltNet mailing list discussion group over the years. Some very good ideas!

> **T**
> **I**
> **P**
>
> *Looking for someone to repair your antique quilt?* Visit **The Quilt Doctor (http://www.quiltdoctor.com)**. Established in 1987 in Washington, D.C., The Quilt Doctor is dedicated to repairing, finishing, and preserving your quilts. You'll also find supplies for cleaning and storing quilts.

Warning! Beware of E-mail Offers to Make Money by Assembling Crafts at Home

"Would you like to assemble crafts at home and get paid? Be your own boss! Top pay! Earn hundreds of dollars weekly! You can choose from—Beaded Accessories–up to $350.00 Weekly!—Holiday Crafts–up to $270.00 Weekly!—Hair Accessories–up to $320.00 Weekly!" It's one of the most rampant Internet scams. You get an E-mail message promising you hundreds of dollars a week for assembling simple craft items. The catch? You need to buy a craft kit, usually for a hundred dollars or more. Once you assemble the items the company tells you your work is unsatisfactory—but you can keep assembling and sending them more items if you wish. Needless to say, your work is never satisfactory. And the craft items that you're supposed to assemble are so time-intensive, such as beaded hair bands, that no one could ever make a living making and selling them.

Web Sites of Quilting Magazines & free Quilting E-zines

Many quilting magazines host Web sites, where they publish smatterings of articles and patterns from current issues. But in addition to "newsstand" quilting magazines, you will also find on the Web electronic magazines, or "E-zines" in cyber-speak. These are magazines you'll read nowhere else. Some are humble efforts that are distributed via E-mail. Others are lavish displays featuring quilts, hotlinks, and snazzy graphics which put their newsstand counterparts to shame. Here's a guide to both the Web sites of major quilting magazines and quilting E-zines.

Free Web Sites for Newsstand Quilt Magazines

PIECEWORK
http://www.interweave.com/needle/piecework.cfm

You'll find a list of the contents of feature stories in this gorgeous Interweave magazine about the history and culture of needlework.

QUILTMAKER
http://www.quiltmaker.com/qm/index.htm

Download free quilting motifs and patterns from this preeminent magazine.

McCALL'S QUILTING
http://www.mccallsquilting.com/mccalls

Tap into articles, patterns, and interviews from the magazine.

McCALL'S QUILTING QUICK QUILTING
http://www.quickquilts.com/qquilts/index.htm

Tap into lessons, patterns, and features from the magazine.

QUILTER'S NEWSLETTER MAGAZINE
http://www.quiltersnewsletter.com/qnm

© 2001 Quilter's Newsletter Magazine

Tap into free patterns, feature articles, calendar news, and "Web Extras"—fun stuff not found in the print publication.

QUICK & EASY QUILTING
http://www.qandequilting.com

Free patterns and features from the magazine.

FONS AND PORTER'S FOR THE LOVE OF QUILTING
http://www.fonsandporter.com/smqmag.html

AMERICAN PATCHWORK AND QUILTING
http://www.bhglive.com/crafts/apq/toc.html

QUILT WORLD
http://www.quilt-world.com

ART QUILT MAGAZINE
http://www.artquiltmag.com

Lynn Lewis Young publishes a gorgeous quarterly magazine devoted to art quilting.

QUILTING ARTS
http://www.quiltingarts.com

This gorgeous new publication is devoted to embellished quilts.

THE QUILTER MAGAZINE
(PREVIOUSLY *TRADITIONAL QUILTER*)
http://www.thequiltermag.com

You'll find free patterns, projects, a quilt store directory and more at this wonderful site.

QUILT TOWN USA
http://www.quilttownusa.com

Quilters will recognize Chitra Publications, home of Quilting Today, Traditional Quiltworks, Miniature Quilts, *and other quilting publications.*

DOWN UNDER QUILTS
http://www.duquilts.com.au

Read what Australian quilters are up to at this marvelous site sponsored by Down Under Quilts *magazine.*

THE PROFESSIONAL QUILTER
http://www.professionalquilter.com

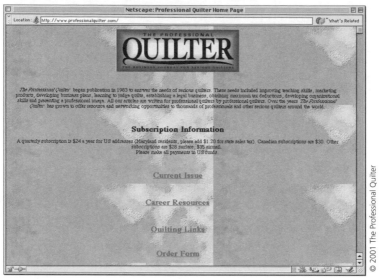

This quarterly publication is dedicated to the needs of serious quilters—and features the hottest articles on computer quilting (many written by Gloria).

More Free Web Sites of Magazines Quilters Will Enjoy

THREADS MAGAZINE
http://www.taunton.com/th

Threads *offers a wide selection of how-to articles and tips from the magazine, with a searchable index.*

SEW NEWS
http://www.sewnews.com

You'll find lots of great articles online, including a searchable index and articles from back issues.

BELLE ARMOIRE—ART TO WEAR
http://www.bellearmoire.com

This magazine showcases unique wearable art projects.

FIBERARTS—THE MAGAZINE OF TEXTILES
http://www.fiberartsmagazine.com

Selected feature articles, a calendar page, profiles, and review are included.

BETTER HOMES & GARDENS
http://www.bhg.com

This site is loaded with how-tos, projects, and feature articles for every area of your home.

AMERICA'S FAVORITE QUILTING MAGAZINES
http://www.quiltmag.com

This is the home of Quilt Almanac, Quilt, Miniature Quilt Ideas, Country Quilts, *and* Big Block Quilts. *The magazines offer lessons, patterns, and tips online.*

T I P

Looking for a Back Issue of an Old Quilting Magazine? You saw it on a newsstand back in 1978—a quilting magazine with a terrific pattern for a pieced, bed-sized hibiscus. But for some reason you didn't buy it, and now you'd give anything for a copy of that magazine. Can you find it on the Web? Yup. Head to **Bette Feinstein's Hard to Find Needlework Books (http://www.needle workbooks.com)**. Bette offers a wide selection of old stitch-ing magazines, as well as out of print books. Drop Bette a note if you can't find the magazine you're looking for on her site. Then head to the Web flea market **eBay (http://www.ebay.com)**. You'll find hundreds of quilting magazines and patterns up for sale. Use the main searcher to search for the title of the magazine. And be sure to check the service every few days because items up for sale change fast.

Free (or Nearly Free) Electronic Quilting Magazines

WEBTHREADS
http://www.welshofer.com/WebThreads

This free E-zine by Sehoy L. Welshofer is a real treat. Sehoy covers everything from quilting software to reviews of new quilting books.

COMPUTER QUILTING BYTES
http://softexpressions.com/help/newsletters

Sharla Hicks offers a free newsletter filled with tips and techniques relating to computing quilters.

Find Other Magazines You Like on the Web
As we said, just about every magazine runs its own Web site. To find the ones you're interested in head to the publication lists of one of the major searchers like **Yahoo!** (**http://www.yahoo.com/News/Magazines/**). Or, check out these magazine sites:

HEARST HOME ARTS
http://homearts.com

You'll find all the Hearst home-oriented magazines here including Victoria, Country Living, Good Housekeeping, *and* Redbook. *You can read selections from all, plus special features written for the Web.*

MARTHA STEWART LIVING
ttp://www.marthastewart.com

Martha Stewart fans will find show schedules and upcoming news on books and Martha Stewart Living.

COUNTRY COLLECTIBLES
http://www.countrycollector.com

Read stories from the magazine, plus find craft projects including ones for quilting

---

CELIA EDDY'S QUILTSTORY
http://www.quilt.co.uk

This lovely British publication from Celia Eddy offers quilting news, articles, reviews, and more. It's also an excellent place to learn about quilt-related events happening in the UK.

QUILTZINE
http://www.auntie.com/qzine

The Auntie-Dot-Com posts an E-zine that includes projects and patterns, and tells you what's new on the Auntie craft site.

NINE PATCH NEWS
http://hometown.aol.com/ninepatchn/index.html

From America Online's quilting forum comes a newsletter written by AOL quilters. Topics are chatty and cover topics ranging from use of masking tape to shopping trip experiences. You can read it on the Web site or get it via E-mail.

JUDY MARTIN'S FREE ONLINE NEWSLETTER
http://www.judymartin.com/newsletter/index.html

Read Judy's past newsletters or subscribe to have new issues delivered to your E-mail box.

THE VIRTUAL QUILTER
http://www.planetpatchwork.com/news.htm

Rob Holland writes the most audacious quilting E-zine on the Web. Best of all, it's free! Peruse the index, request a free sample, or subscribe.

QUILTERS' NUGGETS NEWSLETTER
http://quilting.about.com/library/weekly/blQNuggt.htm

You can get a free weekly newsletter from Quilting at About.Com, hosted by Susan Druding. The newsletter tells you what's new on the site.

THE QUILT GALLERY MAGAZINE
http://www.quiltgallery.com

This is an amazing and beautiful free online publication devoted to contemporary quilting. It offers an online discussion area and E-mail notification of new issues.

SHARON DARLING'S QUILTER'S REVIEW
http://quiltersreview.com

Find out what other quilters think about marking pencils, scissors, quilt basting spray, and quilting books.

THE QUILTING CONSUMER
http://www.tvq.com/qconsume.htm

Before making an investment in a quilting product, tap into Quilting Consumer for some informed advice.

MARSHA MCCLOSKEY'S FREE NEWSLETTER
http://quilt.com/MarshaMcCloskey

Sign up for a free newsletter by tapping into this Web site.

FIBERNEWS HOME PAGE
http://hometown.aol.com/FiberNews/fibernews.html

You'll enjoy this monthly E-mail newsletter for fiber arts enthusiasts by Lili Pintea-Reed. There is a small subscription fee, but a free issue and some articles are available for reading at the Web site.

AMI SIMM'S FREE NEWSLETTER
http://www.MalleryPress.com/Artists/AmiSimms/Free Newsletter.html ·

Ami starting sending newsletters in January 1997 as a follow-up to her monthly chats on America Online. Back issues filled with Ami's wit and wisdom are available to read on the Web site, or sign up for a monthly issue to arrive in your E-mail.

**T
I
P**

Find More Quilt Magazines
Like fat quarters, you can never have enough of them—subscriptions to quilt magazines, that is. When you tire of reading them on the Web subscribe to them by mail. On Sue Traudt's World Wide Quilting page you'll find a **"Quilt Magazine FAQ"** (**http://ttsw.com/FAQS/QuiltMagazineFAQ.html**) compiled from messages written by quilters on which magazines they like, which ones they don't. It includes a list of addresses and subscription information for quilt magazines. Dawn Duperault also offers a list of quilt magazines and their addresses (**http://www.reddawn.net/quilt/magazine.htm**).

free Information on Guilds, Organizations, Contests & Shows

Even though quilters meet through their computers, they still love to get together in each others' living rooms. Many quilting guilds host their own Web pages. Some are austere, offering only membership information, while others are vast networks offering information on upcoming shows, galleries of members' quilts, and information on local shopping (making them good sites to tap into when you're traveling).

Many national quilting and needlework organizations also host Web sites offering information on activities and membership. Lots of quilting contests also advertise through Web sites. We've included at the end of this chapter Web sites that offer directories of these contests.

▒ Free Directories of Local Quilting Guilds

WORLD WIDE QUILTING'S GUILDS AROUND THE WORLD
http://ttsw.com/QuiltGuildsPage.html

Looking for a quilting guild in your neighborhood? Tap into Sue Traudt's quilt guild directory which lists guilds in the United States, Canada, Europe, and Australia. It also includes ideas for guild quilting challenges and activities.

DAWN DUPERAULT'S QUILT GUILDS ONLINE
http://www.reddawn.net/quilt/guilds.htm

Dawn offers an exhaustive list of state quilting guilds around the country, plus links to their Web sites.

BETTER HOMES AND GARDENS'
QUILT GUILD LOCATOR
http://www.bhg.com/quiltvillage/guilds
http://www.quiltvillage.com

Find a quilt guild in your community by tapping into QuiltVillage.Com.

QUILTING GUILDS AROUND THE WORLD
FROM THE QUILT BROKER
http://www.quiltbroker.com/guilds.html

A guide and links to the Web sites of quilting guilds the world over.

QUILT GUILDS AROUND THE WORLD
http://www.quiltguilds.com

You'll find quilt guilds from Guam, South Africa, all fifty states in the U.S., Australia, New Zealand, and other countries in this directory. There is also a guide to quilt shows.

CANADIAN QUILT GUILDS DIRECTORY
http://quilt.com/Guilds/QuiltGuildsCanada.html

Tap into **C&T's Ultimate Directory** to search for a quilting guild or store in your community or the city to which you're traveling. Head to **http://www.ctpub.com** and click on Ultimate Directory.

Tap into the Quilt Guild Web Ring Many quilt guild Web sites are linked by a Web ring. In order to surf the ring you don't actually have to join it. You merely head to the Web ring logo at the bottom of a member page and click your way to the next member pages in the ring. To start, head to the central page at: **http://nav.webring.yahoo.com/hub?ring=quiltguild**.

Web Sites of National Quilting Organizations

AMERICAN QUILTER'S SOCIETY
http://www.AQSquilt.com

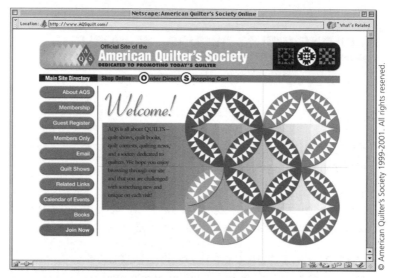

The Web site of this venerable quilting society offers information on membership, shows, and the society's museum.

AMERICAN QUILT STUDY GROUP
http://catsis.weber.edu/aqsg

The American Quilt Study group, founded by Sally Garoutte, is devoted to the study of old quilts and their stories.

THE NATIONAL QUILTING ASSOCIATION
http://www.nqaquilts.org

You can find out how to join this esteemed society, and obtain information on its annual show.

THE ARTQUILT NETWORK
http://www.adkey.com/aqn

THE CRAZY QUILT SOCIETY
http://www.crazyquilt.com

The Crazy Quilt Society, a program of the Quilt Heritage Foundation, is devoted to the study of crazy quilts.

INTERNATIONAL QUILT STUDY CENTER
http://quiltstudy.unl.edu

IQS, located at the University of Nebraska, Lincoln, promotes the study of quilt-making and traditions. The center also hosts a quilt museum.

CONTEMPORARY QUILTART ASSOCIATION
http://www.contemporaryquiltart.com

STUDIO ART QUILT ASSOCIATES
http://www.saqa.com

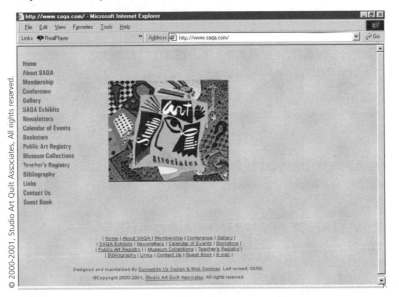

Studio Art Quilt Associates is a national organization for art quilters, and also dealers, teachers, curators, and collectors.

AMERICAN SEWING GUILD
http://www.asg.org

 THE NATIONAL CRAFT ASSOCIATION
http://www.craftassoc.com

The NCA offers lots and lots of crafting tips on its Web site. You'll also find pages on craft show ideas, selling crafts, resources for quilting and sewing, a free newsletter, a chat room, and more.

THE APPLIQUÉ SOCIETY
http://www.theappliquesociety.org

THE ALLIANCE FOR AMERICAN QUILTS
http://www.quilts.org/alliance.htm

THE ART QUILT NETWORK
http://www.adkey.com/aqn

Free Information on International Guilds and Organizations

THE INTERNATIONAL QUILT ASSOCIATION
http://www.quilts.org/iqa.htm

INTERNATIONAL MACHINE QUILTERS ASSOCIATION
http://www.imqa.org

THE WEST AUSTRALIAN QUILTER'S ASSOCIATION
http://members.tripod.com/waqa

BELGIUM PATCHWORK ASSOCIATION
http://www.belgiumquilt.be

CANADIAN QUILTERS ASSOCIATION
http://www.canadianquilter.com

THE LONDON QUILTERS
http://members.tripod.co.uk/London_Quilters/lq1.htm

You'll find here links to other UK quilting sites and a list of London area quilt stores.

THE QUILT ACADEMY OF SWEDEN
http://home5.swipnet.se/~w-58758

PATCHWORK GUILD OF AUSTRIA
http://members.magnet.at/patchfan/pwga_e.htm

FRENCH PATCHWORK
http://www.francepatchwork.com

Free Directories of Quilting Contests, Shows, and Symposiums

More and more quilt shows and contests are advertising through Web sites. We couldn't include them all, but here are sites for many large shows and directories to the ever-changing universe of shows and contests.

WORLD WIDE QUILTING'S QUILT EXHIBITIONS AND MUSEUMS
http://quilt.com/Museums.html

Sue Traudt maintains a directory of links to the Web sites of quilt shows, contests, classes—and even cruises. She has also included quilt show reviews submitted by visitors to her site.

QUILTS, INC. QUILT SHOW GUIDE
http://www.quilts.com

Tap into the Web site of the creators of the spring and fall Quilt Markets, and other big international quilt shows, for schedules and information.

QUILT FESTIVALS BY MANCUSO, INC.
http://www.quiltfest.com

You'll find here links to Williamsburg Festival Week, World Quilt & Textile show, Pennsylvania National Quilt Extravaganza, and Pacific International Quilt Festival.

QUILTING IN THE TETONS
http://www.quiltthetetons.org

VERMONT QUILT FESTIVAL
http://www.vqf.org

If you're planning on going to the Quilter's Heritage Celebration in Lancaster, Pennsylvania, be sure to check out **Judy Smith's Lancaster County, PA Area Resources for Quilters (http://www.quiltart.com/ lancaster.html**). Judy includes a map and the best shops of interest to quilters, and directions how to get there.

QUILTING BY THE LAKE
http://www.quiltingbythelake.com

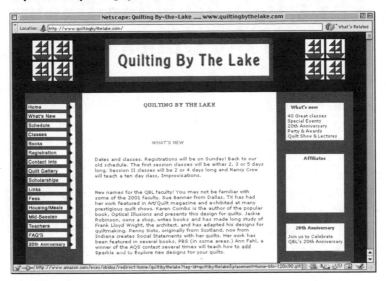

QUILTER'S QUEST WORKSHOPS
http://www.quiltersquest.com

QUILTER'S HERITAGE CELEBRATION
http://www.qhconline.com

NATIONAL QUILTING ASSOCIATION'S
ANNUAL SHOW
http://www.nqaquilts.org

AMERICAN QUILTER'S SOCIETY ANNUAL SHOW
http://www.AQSquilt.com

MINNESOTA QUILTS ANNUAL SHOW
http://www.mnquilt.org/annual_shows.htm

WORLD WIDE QUILTING'S QUILT SHOWS AROUND
THE WORLD
http://ttsw.com/QuiltShowsPage.html

free Help Tracking Down an Old Quilt's History

One of the most frequently asked questions on the Internet is "How can I restore my grandma's quilt?" The first step is to date the quilt and unriddle the nature of the fabrics she used. Is it a calico from a work apron? Twill from a Confederate soldier's uniform? The second step is to find reproduction and vintage fabrics to patch those worn blocks (if you wish).

Or maybe you don't have an old quilt to repair. Perhaps you're merely interested in the history of quilting—and other needlearts as well. Many Web sites offer articles on quilting history. The articles often include photos of antique quilts and links to other quilting history spots on the Internet.

Free Quilt History Discussions to Join

QUILT HERITAGE MAILING LIST
http://www.quilthistory.com

The Quilt History Web site offers articles, links, and fun related to quilt history. You can also sign up for a mailing list discussion group. Send a subscribe request to QHL-request@cuenet.com. To obtain the digest version send a request to QHL-Digest-request@cuenet.com. To post a message to the group, send a note to QHL@cuenet.com.

TIP

Visit Textiles Museums on the Web
Stop in at **Marsha White's Textiles Through Time** (**http://www.interlog.com/~gwhite/ttt/tttintro.html**) for links to all the best textiles museums in cyberspace.

▦ Web Sites with Quilt History Information

THE LIBRARY OF CONGRESS: AMERICAN MEMORY
http://lcweb2.loc.gov

Search on the word "quilt" and this amazing Web site will serve up a list of oral-history interviews with quilters conducted by the WPA work project during the Depression. You can also view photos of old quilts from the library's archives.

WORLD WIDE QUILTING HISTORY PAGE
http://quilt.com/QuiltHistoryPage.html

Sue Traudt offers wonderful information on the history of quilting around the world, the origin of different quilting styles, and the stories behind different blocks and techniques.

QUILTS AND QUILTMAKING IN AMERICA 1978–1996
http://memory.loc.gov/ammem/qlthtml/qlthome.html

This site features quilts from two American Folklife Center collections, the Blue Ridge Parkway Folklife Project Collection and the "All-American Quilt Contest" sponsored by Coming Home, a division of Lands' End, and Good Housekeeping.

INTRODUCTION TO A VICTORIAN WOMAN'S WORLD
http://www.spiritone.com/~zsk

This site, maintained by Zsuzsa Sztaray, is practically an electronic magazine, with scads of interesting articles on the nineteenth-century woman's role in the home and beyond. Among its fare: articles on the decorative arts, holidays of yesteryear, and many, many links to other Victoriana sites on the Web.

🛒 RJR FABRICS
http://www.rjrfabrics.com

RJR Fabrics manufactures many historical reproduction fabric lines well-known to quilters, like the Smithsonian Quilt Fabric Collection, or those based upon fabrics in well-known antique quilts. Its site offers considerable information on the history of quilts, and quilting in particular periods like the 1930s. Its historical information is organized to accompany descriptions of its fabric lines, so head to those when you tap into this lovely site.

DAWN DUPERAULT'S TIMELINE OF QUILTING HISTORY IN AMERICA
http://www.reddawn.net/quilt/timeline.htm

Here's a fascinating page! Dawn traces the history of quilting from pre-colonial Europe into the 1970s. Did you know that in the 1920s blocks colored with Crayons and heat-set were popular? Or that in the 1900s mills perfected the ability to make battings without cotton seed particles stuck in it? Dawn includes an extensive bibliography.

HAWAIIAN QUILT HISTORY
http://www.nvo.com/poakalani/historyofhawaiianquilting/

KATHLEEN DYER'S HISTORICAL AND CULTURAL REFERENCES
http://www.dnai.com/~kdyer/history.html

Kathleen Dyer offers links to a variety of sites around the Internet that offer articles on the history of different kinds of needlework, especially embroidery, lace, and crochet.

ＮＯTES ON QUILT HISTORY
FROM THE QUILTBEE DISCUSSION MAILING LIST
http://www.quiltersbee.com/qbqhisto.htm

This is a collection of messages pertaining to quilting history collected from the QuiltBee discussion list. (See Chapter 3 to learn how to join the discussion group.)

HISTORY OF SOUTHERN QUILTING
http://xroads.virginia.edu/~UG97/quilt/opening.html

The University of Virginia offers a large repository of articles tracing the different influences found in southern quilts, from European to African.

WOMENFOLK, A GATHERING PLACE FOR WOMEN
http://www.womenfolk.com

You'll find numerous articles about the history of fiber arts, including quilting, on this lovely and welcoming Web site for women by Ann Johnson.

"SURVIVING THE WINTER: THE EVOLUTION OF QUILTMAKING AMONG TWO CULTURES IN NEW MEXICO" BY DOROTHY ZOPF
http://www.sla.purdue.edu/WAAW/Zopf/index.html

THE CARON COLLECTION:
THE HISTORY OF CRAZY QUILTING, PART 1
http://www.caron-net.com/featurefiles/featmay.html

THE HISTORY OF CRAZY QUILTING, PART II
http://www.caron-net.com/featurefiles/featmay2.html

Threadmaker Caron Collection offers a feature by Betty Pillsbury and Rita Vainius on the history of this Victorian fad.

QUILTING HISTORY LESSONS AT ABOUT.COM
http://quilting.about.com

Susan Druding offers regular articles on quilt history in About.Com's quilt forum.

DEAR JANE QUILTS
http://www.dearjane.com

This Web site from Brenda Papadakis is dedicated to Jane Stickle and her quilt of 1863 which features 225 quilt patterns. Learn about the quilt and how to make the patterns. There's also a mailing list that you can join and talk to other quilters making Dear Jane quilts.

PLANET PATCHWORK
http://planetpatchwork.com

Rob Holland's Planet Patchwork Web site is well-known among quilters on the Web for serving up compelling articles, many on quilt history. Here are a few:

- **"CIVIL WAR QUILT REVEALS DEEPENING MYSTERY" BY ROB HOLLAND**
http://planetpatchwork.com/cwquilt.htm

- **"A BRIEF HISTORY OF THE FEED SACK" BY JEAN CLARK STAPEL**
http://planetpatchwork.com/feedsack.htm

- **"BUYING OLD QUILTS" BY DEBORAH ROBERTS**
http://planetpatchwork.com/buyqlts.htm

"BLACK HERITAGE VIBRANTLY SHOWN IN QUILTS"
BY JULIE STOEHR
http://www.dailyaztec.com/archive/1996/02/08/file005.html

"QUILTING: THE FABRIC OF WOMEN'S HISTORY"
BY TERRI BITTNER
http://www.suite101.com/article.cfm/womens_history/9160

"MICHIGAN'S AFRICAN-AMERICAN QUILTERS"
BY MARSHA MAC DOWELL AND LYNNE SWANSON
http://www.sos.state.mi.us/history/museum/techstuf/civilwar/
  quiltmag.html

REDWORK HISTORY
http://www.redworklady.com/lectures.htm

"HMONG QUILTS—PA NDAU—
REFLECT HMONG HISTORY" BY JEAN H. LEE
http://www.hmongnet.org/culture/pandau2.html

ANTEBELLUM QUILTS FROM
THE UPPER SHENANDOAH VALLEY
http://www.village.virginia.edu/vshadow2/quilts/quilt.html

View a collection of quilts from the mid-1800s from an exhibition held at the Woodrow Wilson Birthplace and Museum.

> 🛒 *Looking for historically accurate fabrics to use in restoring an old quilt?* Try **Patchworks** (**http://www.reproductionfabrics.com**). They sell cotton reproduction quilting fabrics categorized by historical periods. Patchworks offers a free newsletter you can subscribe to with information on fabric history, new reproduction fabric lines, and special sales.

"QUILTING: A HISTORY"
FROM CRANSTON PRINT WORKS
http://www.cranstonvillage.com/quilt/q-histor.htm

QUILT AND SILK
http:www.quiltandsilk.com

Click the Silk Story link to learn the fascinating history of silk weaving in Lyon.

MICHIGAN HISTORICAL MUSEUM'S PAINT A QUILT
http://www.sos.state.mi.us/history/museum/techstuf/civilwar/
  quilt.html

You'll learn about Civil War quilts at this fun Web site, and if you're a teacher you'll find lots of classroom ideas to get your students inter-ested in both the Civil War and quilts that tell its story.

AMERICAN QUILTS
http://www.americanquilts.com/glossary.htm

American Quilts, which sells USA-made quilts, offers a glossary of antique quilt terms. For instance, "popped" refers to a broken thread or a binding not attached in a small place. A "pristine" quilt is one that has not been washed or used. American Quilts also sells "cutter" quilts which are worn quilts that can be fashioned into other things like pillows.

▦ Free Information About Quilt History and Preservation Societies

THE AMERICAN QUILT STUDY GROUP
http://www2.h-net.msu.edu/~aqsg

The American Quilt Study Group, founded by a klatch of quilt histori-ans in California, is dedicated to researching the stories of quilts and quilt-makers. The organization publishes a journal and newsletter, and sponsors seminars. Membership is $35.

THE ALLIANCE FOR AMERICAN QUILTS
http://www.quilts.org/alliance.htm

Read how to join this organization which seeks to preserve the history of American quilting by linking the resources of libraries and museums, together with the quilting memories and patterns of quilters.

THE QUILT STUDY GROUP OF AUSTRALIA
http://quilt.com/History/AustralianQuiltStudy.html

Devoted to promoting interest and research into quiltmaking in Australia.

Are You a Garage Sale Hound? Do You Love Riffling through Piles of Old Linens at Estate Sales? You'll *love* the Internet flea market site **eBay** (**http://www.ebay.com**). You can bid on old quilts, old fabric, old sewing notions and patterns—anything you'd find at garage sale, even jars of buttons. It's absolutely amazing what you find for sale at this site—and often for bargain prices.

Sales are definitely caveat emptor, since items are offered for sale by individuals around the country, and usually all you know about them is their E-mail address. Are you likely to be fleeced? It depends upon what you bid on. Judy has bought lots of old junk—from vintage clothing to kitschy curtain tiebacks from the '40s. But she usually keeps her purchases under $10.

free Sewing Machine Help

We quilters love our sewing machines. We use them, collect them, display them in our living rooms and shops. But where do you go when you need help mastering that computerized Bernina? Who do you ask when you want to restore that antique Singer Featherweight? The Internet should be your first stop, for information on cleaning and restoring sewing machines, both antique and new, abounds. You'll find manuals for antique sewing machines available for downloading. If you're a fan of antique stitchers you'll find lots of other enthusiasts. Or, if you're merely in the market for a new sewing machine or serger, you'll find advice for shopping.

Quiltropolis (**http://www.quiltropolis.com**) runs numerous mailing list discussion groups devoted to the use of different brands of sewing machines. Among them are ones for Berninas, Janomes, Vikings, Pfaffs, Singer Xls, and Brother PCs. Quiltropolis also runs discussion groups devoted to free motioning quilting and quilting with a long-arm machine. (By the way, scroll down Quiltropolis's Web page and click Ask Martie to read Martie Sandell's features on sewing machine needles, thread, and assorted machine talk.)

A number of sewing Web sites host bulletin boards where talk about different brands of sewing machines is lively. Our favorites include the discussion boards at **Nancy Zieman's Nancy's Notions** (**http://www.nancysnotions.com**) and **Sewing World.Com** (**http://www.sewingworld.com**).

The Web sites of *Threads* (**http://www.taunton.com**) and *Sew News* (**http://www.sewnews.com**) are also terrific places to read articles on the latest trends in sewing machines and snag tips on keeping yours running smoothly. You can find *Sew News'* library at: **http://www.sewnews.com/library.htm**. For *Threads'* head to: **http://www.taunton.com/th/admin/techniques.htm**.

▦ Free Sewing Machine Buying Advice

PURCHASING A SEWING MACHINE FAQ
FROM QUILTNET
http://www.quilt.com/FAQS/SewMachinePurchaseFAQ.html

MACHINE QUILTING NEWS
FROM THE WORLD WIDE QUILTING WEB SITE
http://ttsw.com/Tools/MachineQuiltingNews.html

"SELECTING A SEWING MACHINE"
BY CAROL THAYER
http://www.ianr.unl.edu/pubs/consumered/nf110.htm

"SELECTING A SEWING MACHINE"
FROM THE HOME SEWING ASSOCIATION
http://www.sewing.org/educate/machine.html

THE USENET TEXTILE FAQ
ftp://rtfm.mit.edu/pub/usenet/news.answers/crafts/textiles/faq/part1

The first part of this frequently asked question file assembled from messages posted to the textile crafts newsgroups addresses choices in buying a machine.

❗ TIP

In the Market for a "Previously Driven" Sewing Machine? Visit **Mary Field's Sewing Rummage (http://www.jps.net/cfield/rummage)** to read classified ads for second hand sewing machines and accessories. Also, check out the rummage at **eBay (http://www.ebay.com)**, the Internet flea market where you can find anything old and battered that your heart desires. This is also a great place to hunt for toy sewing machines and sewing machine attachments, especially for vintage models.

THE SEWING FAQ
http://www.skepsis.com/~tfarrell/textiles/sewing

Tom Farrell and Paulo Ruffino have collected these messages posted by members of the Usenet textile newsgroups. It offers information on buying, plus advice on threads and free motion stitching.

🛒 RESOURCES FOR LONG-ARM MACHINE QUILTERS FROM HOUSE OF HANSON
http://www.houseofhanson.com/longarm.html

DEBBIE COLGROVE'S SEWING MACHINE BUYING TIPS AT ABOUT.COM
http://sewing.about.com

 *Free Help Repairing, Maintaining and "Psychoanalyzing" a Sewing Machine*

🛒 "SEWING MACHINE TROUBLESHOOTING GUIDE" BY SINGER SEWING & VACUUM, NJ
http://www.sewingandvac.com/tshoot.htm

"SALVAGING SEWING MACHINES FROM WATER DAMAGE" BY COLLIER (FL) COUNTY EMERGENCY MANAGEMENT
http://www.naples.net/govern/county/emrgmgt/sewing.htm

"WHAT YOU OUGHT TO KNOW ABOUT SEWING MACHINE NEEDLES" BY ROSE MARIE TONDL OF THE UNIVERSITY OF NEBRASKA EXTENSION
http://www.ianr.unl.edu/pubs/textiles/nf250.htm

Free Help for Lovers of Antique Sewing Machines

TREADLE ON
http://www.quiltropolis.net/maillists/maillists.asp

This E-mail-based discussion group is hosted by Quiltropolis and is dedicated to the use, rather than merely the collecting of treadle and hand-cranked sewing machines.

FEATHERWEIGHT FANATICS HOME PAGE
http://quilt.com/fwf

Find out how to learn the birthday of your Singer. There's also a database of pictures of Featherweights (you can add yours if you wish), all courtesy of Sue Traudt and the World Wide Quilting page. Sue also runs the wonderful Featherweight Fanatics for fans of the Singer Featherweight. A modest subscription fee is required. You can read the list's message archives at this site as well as sign up.

INTERNATIONAL SEWING MACHINE COLLECTORS SOCIETY
http://www.ismacs.net

Make this your first stop in your hunt for the genealogy of your antique sewing machine. You'll find answers to questions such as "When was my machine made?" and "What is my machine worth?" For information about specific machines, head to the drop-down menu to read an assortment of articles reprinted from ISMACS Magazine.

TANGLED THREADS
ANTIQUE SEWING MACHINE FAQ
http://kbs.net/tt/faq/index.html

Melissa Bishop and Kapur Business Systems tells you "What is a Featherweight anyway?" with historical information, serial number help, plus advice on restoring antique machines.

> ### !TIP
>
> ### Bargain-Hunt for Collectible Sewing Machines on the Web
>
> You can hunt garage sale-style for antique sewing machines and collectibles, like old manuals, attachments, and bobbins at the **eBay** Web auction site (**http://www.ebay.com**). You'll find for sale on the site an especially large number of toy and miniature sewing machines.

GAILEE'S FEATHERWEIGHT RESOURCE PAGE
http://www.gpbwebworks.com/fwinfo/

Dale and Deloris Pickens, collaborating with Nancy Slater and participants in the Featherweight Fanatics E-mail discussion group, have compiled a treasure chest of advice on Featherweights, from information on bobbin cases, to oiling, cleaning, and maintenance of belts, lights, and foot pedals.

FEATHERWEIGHT FACTS FROM PLANET PATCHWORK
http://www.tvq.com/fweight.htm

Rob Holland continues on the tradition of the Internet "cult of the Featherweight," as he calls it, with his own collection of facts, stories, and links.

SINGER SEWING COMPANY INFORMATION I'VE GATHERED
http://www-persona.umich.edu/%7Esherlyn/singer.html

Sherlyn at the University of Michigan offers a collection of information on vintage Singers.

TREADLE ON INFORMATION CENTRAL
http://www.captndick.com

Stop in at the home page of "Captain Dick" Wightman where you can indulge your love of "Treadleonia" with machine information, a cyber-museum of machines, and a flea market of treadle-related stuff.

"ANTIQUE AND VINTAGE SEWING MACHINES" BY ALAN QUINN
http://www.demon.co.uk/quinn

Alan offers pictures of over 90 different sewing machine models, plus information on shuttle types, like hybrid (transverse/vibrating), oscillating, rotary, plus lots of links to related Web sites.

BOB BANNEN'S SEW 2 GO.COM
http://www.sew2go.com

Are you looking for a Singer Featherweight, or perhaps a toy sewing machine? Check out this Web site for information and sales. Threading instructions and diagrams for over 100 vintage and antique machines are available for a small fee, and some are available to download for free.

TIP

You Can Find on the Net Just About Any Sewing Manual Ever Printed If you're hunting for a manual for that 1942 Singer you hauled in from the neighbor's trash, start your search at the Web site of the **International Sewing Machine Collectors Society (http://www.ismacs.net)**. In the frequently asked questions section of the Web site you'll find a list of vintage sewing machine manuals that can be purchased from Graham Forsdyke (graham@ismacs.net).

If, in the course of your search you discover the machine's not really a Singer but a White, head to **Sewing Manuals, a Look Into the Past (http://www.show.aust.com/~sewing/book.htm)** which sells manuals for any brand of machine. (They claim to have manuals for every sewing machine that's ever been imported into Australia.) Also keep an eye on eBay **(http://www.ebay.com)** because at any given time there will be fifty or more vintage sewing machine manuals for sale—some selling for less than a spool of thread.

---

free Help for Specific Brands of Sewing Machines

A good sewing machine store has no substitute. But talking to other sewers who quilt with the same brand of sewing machine that you do can be immensely helpful. Other quilters can recommend products and attachments. They can offer advice on potentially tricky endeavors like free-motion quilting with metallic thread. They can even help with troubleshooting. We can't recommend strongly enough that you join a mailing list discussion group devoted to your model of sewing machine.

Free Help for Berninas

BERNINA FAN CLUB MAILING LIST
http://quilt.com/BFC

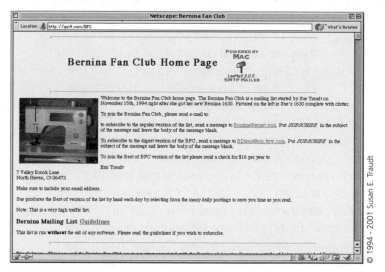

Sue Traudt runs this discussion group which is popular with quilters. From this Web site you can also visit the Web pages of other Bernina fans.

BERNINA 1630
http://www.quiltropolis.net/maillists/maillists.asp

Martie Sandell runs this mailing list sponsored by Quiltropolis. It's for discussing anything related to the Bernina 1630.

BERNINA USA CHATS AND FORUMS
http://www.berninausa.com/letstalk/index.html

Bernina offers regular online chats with Bernina tech support and marketing people, as well as nationally known Bernina sewing book authors and embroidery design experts. You can also tap into bulletin board discussions in the following topics: Artista; Activa/Virtuosa; Bernina 1630s; Crafts and Dolls; Bernina embroidery, heirloom sewing, home dec sewing, serging, and tailoring.

BERNINA QUESTIONS AND ANSWERS
http://www.berninausa.com/qanda/index.html

Bernina offers an easily searchable database of information on their machines.

 Free Help for Brother Machines

BROTHER PC MAILING LIST
http://www.quiltropolis.net/maillists/maillists.asp

Quiltropolis runs this mailing list for owners of the Brother PC.

Free Help for New Home Janome Machines

JANOME NEW HOME FAQ
http://janome.com/faq.html

Sewing machine maker Janome offers answers to lots of common questions like, "When I try to sew a blind hem, I always see too much of my thread in the front of my garment. How can I make smaller stitches?"

HINTS & TIPS FOR NEW HOME/JANOME SEWING MACHINES
http://www.sewingroom.com/store/tiphdr.htm

Stutsman and The Sewing Room offer lots of help, including information on the Scan N Sew PC.

 JANOME NEW HOME MAILING LIST
http://www.quiltropolis.net/maillists/maillists.asp

Quiltropolis runs this discussion group for Janome owners.

 # Free Help for Viking Machines

 **VIKING2SEW MAILING LIST**
http://www.quiltropolis.net/maillists/maillists.asp

Robin Elder runs this mailing list sponsored by Quiltropolis and devoted to discussing Viking sewing machines, sergers, embroidery, customizing and digitizing.

Free Help for Pfaffs

PFAFFIES MAILING LIST
To join this discussion group E-mail: majordomo@embroideryclubs.com. In the message's Subject line type: **subscribe.** *In the message type:* **subscribe pfaffies yourfullname.** *You can read past messages posted to the group by heading to:*

PFAFFERS
http://www.quiltropolis.com/NewMailinglists.asp

This list, run by Pandy Lolos and Susan Druding, is for owners of the 1475, 7550 and 7570 machines. This list is for busy sewers and has strict rules about no chatting or off-topic messages. Using the PC Design software to design embroidery is a focus of the list.

PFAFFIES MAILING LIST ARCHIVES
ftp://listserv.embroideryclubs.com/archives/pfaffies-digest

MARY FIELD'S PFAFF SEWING ROOM
PFAFFPFRIENDS MAILING LIST AND ARCHIVES
http://www.jps.net/cfield/pfaff

*Check out Mary Field's sewing room and subscribe to the
Pfaffpfriends mailing list and read archives of their messages.*

PAULA MILNER'S SEWING AND DACHSHUNDS
http://www.cyberport.net/users/milnerwm

PAULA MILNER'S PFAFFIE FAQ
http://www.cyberport.net/users/milnerwm/FAQ.html

*You'll find information and links to resources around the Net to answer just
about every question you have about your Pfaff. This is a wonderful site!*

PFAFF-TALK BULLETIN BOARD
FOR NON-HOOP MACHINES
http://www.pfaff-talk.com/non-hoop_machines

PFAFF-TALK BULLETIN BOARD FOR HOOP
MACHINES LIKE THE 7570
http://www.pfaff-talk.com/hoop_machines

Free Help for Singer Machines

SINGER XL MAILING LIST
http://www.quiltropolis.net/maillists/maillists.asp

Quiltropolis runs a discussion group for Singer owners.

Web Sites of Sewing Machine Makers

Many manufacturers offer tips, project pages, and extensive resources and information about their machines on their Web sites.

BABY LOCK CANADA
http://www.babylockcanada.com

BERNINA
http://www.berninausa.com

ELNA USA
http://www.elnausa.com

BROTHER
http://www.brother.com

HUSQVARNA VIKING
http://www.husqvarnaviking.com

JANOME NEW HOME
http://www.janome.com

JUKI
http://www.juki.com

MELCO
http://www.melco.com

PFAFF
http://www.pfaff.com

PFAFF AUSTRALIA
http://www.pfaffaustralia.com.au

RICCAR
http://www.riccar.com

SINGER
http://www.singersewing.com

BABY LOCK
http://www.babylock.com

WHITE
http://www.whitesewing.com

free Directories & Patterns for Helping Others with Quilts

There's nothing quilters love more than a quilting charity project. Quilters on the Internet are an especially generous bunch, stitching quilts for sick children and disaster survivors. Here's a guide to some of the quilting and sewing charity projects you can get involved with through the Internet.

PROJECT LINUS
http://www.projectlinus.org

Project Linus has delivered over 265,000 home-made security blankets to pediatric cancer patients and other children in trauma through its chapters throughout the United States. Find out how you can join this effort by stitching up some blankies.

WRAP THEM IN LOVE
http://www.wraptheminlove.org

The Wrap Them In Love Foundation gives quilts to needy children throughout the world. You can see donated quilts on their Web site, and learn how you can participate.

TINY MIRACLES
http://members.aol.com/bukulu/index.html

Ellen Ann Bidigare tells you how you can donate a quilt to Tiny Miracles, a quilt donation drive for hospital neo-natal intensive care units.

Quilting Charity Projects Are Everything in Cyberspace

Many of the quilt mailing lists featured in Chapter 3 also conduct charity projects. Pitching in can be as easy as getting together with your friends via E-mail.

BINKY PATROL
http://www.binkypatrol.org

Quilts and blankets donated to Binky Patrol are distributed to children born with HIV+, or born drug-addicted, or with other serious illnesses. Binky Patrol also gives them to children who are abused, in foster care, or experiencing trauma.

SEWING WITH NANCY'S SEW A SMILE
http://www.nancysnotions.com
http://www.creativekindness.com

Click on the Sewing Room link and select Sew With a Smile *to tap into Nancy Zieman's extensive database of sewing charity projects around the country that are stitching up everything from sleeping bags for kids in homeless shelters to hats and scarves for disaster victims. Nancy offers contact information, plus needs (looking for a charity that could use all that extra fabric in your closet?), and tips for organizing your sewing guild.*

QUILTS FROM CARING HANDS
http://www.reese.org/qch/Default.htm

Over the past ten years QCH has given over 2,000 quilts to homeless children, children in foster care, AIDS-infected children, and other at-risk children.

THE HOME SEWING ASSOCIATION'S CARING AND SHARING

http://www.sewing.org/careshare/index.html

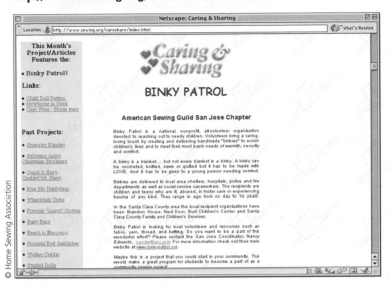

The HSA offers wonderful resources for anyone who wants to use their sewing skills to help those in need in their community. The HSA offers free patterns for chemotherapy turbans, a hospital-bed saddlebag, a walker caddy, "Suzy bags" for mastectomy patients, a lap robe for wheelchair users, preemie "angel" gowns, emergency teddy bears, and more. The HSA also offers advice on organizing group sewing projects, plus Web links and contact information for getting in touch with agencies that need these items.

SEW FOR THE CURE

http://www.sewforthecure.org

Tap into the Web site of this organization founded by the Home Sewing Association. It gathers donations from members of the sewing and craft industry to support foundations active in breast-cancer research. You can make a donation, buy a pin, or send a greeting card to support the cause.

UFO-RPHANAGE FOR QUILTERS
http://www.mindspring.com/~panin/UFO-rphanage

Laura Starr of San Antonio, Texas will take your unfinished quilting projects and convert them into quilts to donate to women's shelters, senior centers, quilts for kids projects, the Pine Ridge Reservation project, churches, and other good causes.

"GOOD WORKS & QUILTING FOR CHARITY" FROM ABOUT.COM
http://quilting.about.com/hobbies/quilting/library/weekly/
aa081997.htm

Susan Druding, quilting guide for About.Com, offers links and information on quilting charity projects around the world.

THE CARE WEAR PATTERN AND INFORMATION SITE
http://www.hood.edu/carewear

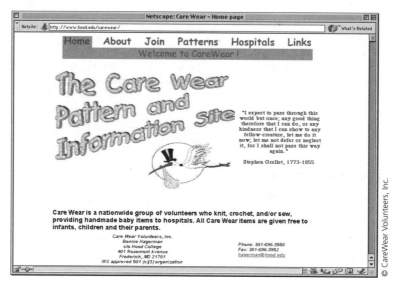

Learn how you can knit, crochet, or sew baby items to give to needy infants, children, and their parents in hospitals. The site includes a directory of free patterns, including ones for bunnies, bears, and more cuddlies.

NEWBORNS IN NEED
http://www.newbornsinneed.com

Newborns In Need stitches clothes, toys, and quilts for sick and needy newborns in hospitals around the country. Tap in to find out if there's a chapter in your area—or how to form one. Read chapter newsletters and order patterns.

1,000 QUILTS FOR OKLAHOMA
http://www.quiltheritage.com/thousand.htm

1,000 DOLLS FOR OKLAHOMA
http://www.quiltheritage.com/thousand-dolls.htm

Learn how you can make quilts and toys for survivors of the Oklahoma tornado at this site run by the Quilt Heritage Foundation.

VICTORIA'S QUILTS
http://home.att.net/~blimper/home.html

Victoria's Quilts sews quilts for cancer patients and cancer treatment facilities.

ABC QUILTS PROJECTS
http://www.abcquilts.org

ABC is a national volunteer group that provides quilts to HIV-infected and abandoned babies in hospitals around the country.

INTERQUILT'S HUGS PROJECT BEARS FOR KIDS
http://kbs.net/tt/hugs.html

*Melissa Bishop's InterQuilt mailing-list discussion group sews bears for children in need. They also offer their preferred bear pattern online, downloadable in Adobe PDF format. Also take a look at the **Tangled Threads Has a Heart** Web page (**http://kbs.net/tt/heart.html**) for more information and links to quilting charity projects around the Web.*

PROJECT WARM FUZZIES
http://warmfuzzies.home.att.net

Project Warm Fuzzies sews quilts to give to children at St. Jude's, the twenty-plus Shriners' hospitals, and other hospitals. (Note that the founder is no longer administering this project from her home; however, she includes a list of contact people for Web site visitors who still want to help.)

HICKORY CORNER QUILTS' GOOD WORKS DIRECTORY
http://www.hickoryhillquilts.com/good_works.htm

Hickory Corner offers a directory with Web links to quilting charity projects.

SUNSHINE FOUNDATION
http://www.sunshinefnd.com

The Sunshine Foundation is a Mennonite affiliated non-profit agency in Maumee, Ohio that provides support services to individuals with developmental disabilities and their families. They auction quilts stitched by Amish and Mennonite communities (and other volunteers) to raise funds for projects for the disabled.

QUILTING WITH CHILDREN FROM HEDDI CRAFT
http://www.thecraftstudio.com/qwc

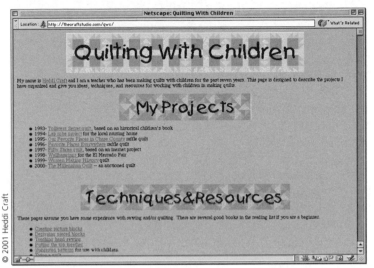

Heddi, a sixth-grade teacher, describes projects and techniques for making quilts with children, including charity quilts.

▦ *Memorial Quilt Projects*

Quilts commemorating cancer victims, victims of child abuse, and other tragedies are wonderful monuments to the human spirit. Visit these Web sites to view memorial quilts, and find out how you can get involved.

RAGING LIGHT PROJECT:
THE BREAST CANCER NAMES BANNER
http://www.quiltart.com/judy/ragingl1.html

Susan Gray started a banner quilted with names of breast cancer victims to be carried to breast cancer fund-raising activities. (The carrying of quilted and embroidered banners has a long history in the woman's suffrage movement.) You can learn how to get involved at this informative site.

BE CAREFUL OF CYBERSPACE PITCHES FOR SYMPATHY

It happens every day. Some normally intelligent stitcher receives an E-mail mass-mailing from someone who is supposedly collecting quilts for some vaguely named charity, or for victims of a disaster recently in the news. Often the E-mail comes with a plea for money. The sympathetic quilter immediately forwards the message to 2,000 of her closest cyber gal-pals.

While many wonderful quilting charity projects flourish in cyberspace, you should regard E-mail requests for your money, sympathy, and quilts with caution. Here are some things to keep in mind:

If you receive an E-mail from someone who is collecting quilts or other goods for victims of a recent disaster, consider whether it wouldn't be wiser to send donations to an established relief agency. Agencies like the Red Cross have personnel in place to get donations directly and quickly to disaster victims. Individuals who collect donations, via the Web, sometimes have no way of getting the items to the disaster victims.

Be skeptical of E-mail pitches from charities you've never heard of. You should also be careful of requests for donations from people who purport that they're collecting goods for some well-known charity, but are not actually affiliated with that organization. Head to the Web sites of the **Better Business Bureau (http://www.bbbonline.org)** to check out charities.

Be skeptical of Web auctions for charities. One often sees, in descriptions of items up for sale on Web auction sites like eBay, a claim that a portion of the proceeds from the sale will go to some animal shelter or whatnot. There is usually no way of verifying that this is true.

Be skeptical of Web shopping sites that claim to donate portions of profits to charities. Usually no more than a few cents of any purchase goes to charity.

If you absolutely must forward an E-mail pitch for donations to all the members of your quilting mailing list, send it first to the list's owner or moderator and ask if the post would be suitable.

While we're on the subject, please delete any E-mail chain letters that request that you to 1) E-mail some government agency to help save the Internet from ill-conceived legislation or save public television from the same; 2) E-mail some company or person because they have promised to donate a penny for every E-mail they receive to some charity; 3) E-mail some kid who's supposedly trying to set a world record for receiving more E-mail than anyone else. In other words, *delete any E-mail chain letter you receive!*

THE BOISE PEACE QUILT PROJECT
http://www.peacequilt.org

The Peace Quilt Project is a group of quilters who stitch quilts to give to world leaders and organizations that have made significant contributions in the realms of peace, justice, and the environment.

CHILD ABUSE QUILTS
http://members.tripod.com/mbgoodman/caq/caq1.html

Several dozen quilters on the mailing list QuiltArt assembled quilts on the theme of child abuse. You can view the quilts at this Web site, and arrange to have the quilts displayed in your community

NIFTY FIFTY QUILTERS BREAST CANCER QUILT
http://hometown.aol.com/Trequilts/charity.html

TWENTY PLENTY BREAST CANCER QUILT
http://hometown.aol.com/trequilts/page6/index.htm

Read about the quilts that these prolific cyber-quilters have assembled to raise money for breast cancer research.

THE BREAST CANCER QUILT PROJECTS
http://www.caron-net.com/galleryfiles/galmay.html

Thread-maker The Caron Collection offers an article on Susan Gray, originator of the "Raging Light" breast cancer quilt project, and Judy Reimer, founder of the "Life Quilt for Breast Cancer" project.

MARY GRAHAM'S
COLUMBINE HIGH MEMORIAL QUILT
http://www.nmia.com/~mgdesign/qor/freepatterns/columbine/
columbine.html

Mary offers a free pattern for a quilt memorializing the students killed in the Littleton, Colorado high school.

THE NAMES PROJECT FOUNDATION:
AIDS MEMORIAL QUILT
http://www.aidsquilt.org/quilt

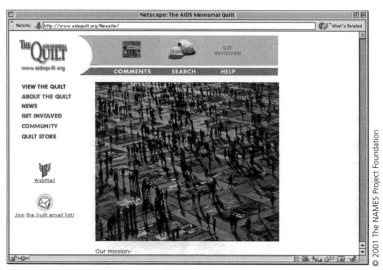

© 2001 The NAMES Project Foundation

See the AIDS quilt online, plus download directions for sewing a commemorative panel.

Add the Name of a Loved One to the Cancer Cyber Quilt

Add the name of a loved one battling cancer, along with a message of support, to the **Cancer Cyber Quilt** (**http://www.wehealnewyork.org/services/cancer/cyberquilt**), a Web site maintained by a consortium of New York hospitals. Or, tap in to read the heartwarming dedications.

Giving Can Be as Simple as Rummaging through Your Closet

Many of these charity sewing projects are eager for donations of fabric, batting, and thread. Head to their Web sites to find out what they need.

Get Fabric Scraps for Your Charity Quilting Project

Could your quilting charity project use fabric scraps of rayon, Dacron, fleece, jersey, and poly-cotton blends? Tap into **Magic Mike's Factory Fabric Scraps Program** (**http://www.nepanetwork.com/magicmik**) to learn how, for the cost of postage and handling, you can get a big box of scraps. Mike Lizonitz from the Wilkes-Barre/ Scranton area of Pennsylvania recycles "cut aways" from area apparel factories by sending them to chari-ties. Since 1995, he has saved over 30,000 pounds of fabric from going into landfills. Tap into this amazing site to learn how you can obtain fabric and to view photos of how others made use of Mike's scraps.

free Help Designing Quilts on a Computer

Thinking of trying to design quilts on your computer, but don't know where to start? You can download demo versions of many quilt designs programs on the Web. You can also download shareware, read reviews of quilt software and link up with other quilters who design quilts on their computers.

Web Sites of Makers of Quilt Design Software

Visit the Web sites of these quilt design software makers for information about their products, downloadable demos, online tutorials and designs, and more.

THE ELECTRIC QUILT COMPANY
http://www.electricquilt.com

At the home of Electric Quilt, Block Base, and Sew Precise you'll find news, patterns, tips, links to EQ "doings" around the Web, plus free clipart. No demos are presently available.

T I P

Why Does that Scanned Fabric Look Different on Your Computer Monitor than It Does When You Print It? Your monitor creates colors through light while your printer creates colors through pigment. Unfortunately the twain often don't meet. Betsy Szymanski authored a good article on using your computer to create colors in quilt design for **Compuquilt** (**http://www.compuquilt.com/rgb.htm**).

BARGELLO DESIGNER
http://www.ayersoft.com

With Bargello Designer by AyerSoft you can create beautiful bargello patterns for quilting. The program works with Windows 95 and later, and a demo is available.

QUILT-PRO SYSTEMS
http://www.quiltpro.com

At the home of quilt design software Quilt-Pro, Foundation Factory, and 1-2-3 Quilt! there's a demo of Quilt-Pro available for both PCs and Macs. You'll also find patterns, tips, lessons, and a mailing list.

QUILTSOFT: SOFTWARE FOR QUILTERS
http://www.quiltsoft.com

You'll find information about QuiltSOFT quilt design software, available for both PCs and Macs, as well as QuiltSOFT fabric CD-ROMs. No demos available.

VQUILT
http://www.vquilt.com

Learn about this quilt design software for PCs from Phil Hisley. Scroll towards the bottom of the page and you'll find Java applets for designing online quilt blocks and tiling patterns.

PC QUILT BY NINA ANTZE
http://www.pcquilt.com

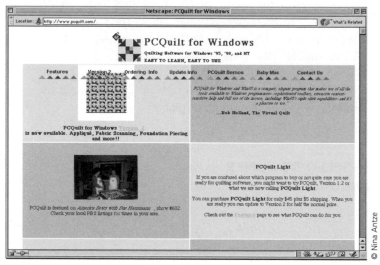

Download demos for both Windows and Mac versions of this quilt designing program, plus sample blocks.

▨ Web Sites With Help for Designing Quilts With Electric Quilt

Electric Quilt and Quilt-Pro are the two most popular quilt designing programs. Web sites and discussion groups for users of these programs abound. We've listed some of the many Web sites for Electric Quilt, and later in this chapter we list Web sites devoted to Quilt-Pro. Along with advice, users of these programs also swap quilt and quilt block designs to use with the programs.

🐝 THE CLUBEQ USERS GROUP
http://members.aol.com/anotherpat/clubeq.html

This group holds challenges, hosts a cyber-gallery of quilts designed with EQ, and can link you up with EQ User's Groups around the world (there's probably one in your state).

EQ PATCH FROM PATCHPIECES
http://www.patchpieces.com/EQpatch.htm

Patti R. Anderson shares Electric Quilt 4 tutorials such as drawing a giant dahlia, skewing blocks into a diamond, drawing a block within a block, Penrose tile quilts, and other ideas.

ELECTRIC QUILT 4 TUTORIAL
ON APPLIQUÉ TRACING
http://myquilts.hypermart.net/eq.htm

Rita Deneberg explains how she scans a drawing and traces it in EQ4 to create an appliqué pattern.

ELECTRIC QUILT TUTORIALS
http://www.quilt-design.com/eq4projectfiles.htm

Ute-Barbara Skjønberg offers lessons on using images as fabric fill, PatchDraw instructions, creating different border sizes, and using the Country Set and layers. She also shares project pages and helpful resourses.

ELECTRIC QUILT 4 QUILTS
http://www.fortunecity.de/kunterbunt/hessen/298/eq4/eq4.htm

Catherine Pascal offers a lesson on how she created a spiral quilt circle based on the 9 degree ruler.

QUILT BUS ELECTRIC QUILT 4 TIPS
http://www.quiltbus.com/EQ%20Tips.htm

JANE AND FRIENDS
http://sites.netscape.net/nanajanec/index.html

Here's a collection of beautiful quilts designed using Electric Quilt.

ELECTRIC QUILT 3 ONLINE LESSONS FROM KAREN COMBS
http://www.karencombs.com/classes.htm

• TRANSPARENT STARS
http://www.wcnet.org/ElectricQuiltCo/kcombs.htm

• TRANSPARENCY IN QUILTS
http://www.wcnet.org/ElectricQuiltCo/kcombs2.htm

• 3D PATCHWORK
http://www.wcnet.org/ElectricQuiltCo/kcombs3.htm

JAN T. EXPLAINS MAKING A SCRAP QUILT USING ELECTRIC QUILT, COURTESY OF DOWN UNDER QUILTERS ONLINE IN AUSTRALIA
http://www.duquilts.com.au/shopping/duqshop/3elect.htm

Web Sites With Help for Designing Quilts With Quilt-Pro

THE QUILT-PRO LIST
http://www.n-stitches.com/QuiltPro/QuiltPro_Support.html

Join this mailing list discussion group to learn how to get the most out of your Quilt-Pro design software.

QUILT-PRO CONNECTION
http://www.n-stitches.com/QuiltPro

You'll find a frequently-asked-question file of information posted to the Quilt-Pro List on everything from adding to designs and drawing curves. There are free block designs to download in the library section.

SHEILA WILLIAMS' QUILTING PAGE
http://www.SheilaWilliams.com/Quilting/Quilting2.html

Sheila offers tutorials for Quilt-Pro 3, as well as Electric Quilt.

HINTS AND TIPS ON HOW TO USE QUILT-PRO
BY FRANK SMITH
http://www.softexpressions.com/help/newsletters/index.html
 #quiltpro

Frank Smith shares a collection of Quilt-Pro tutorials on topics such as drawing symmetrical curved shapes, making custom grids and 3-D blocks, tricks for working with grids that do not line up with patches, switching the snap-to function during the drawing of a patch, and more.

Web Sites Where You Can Download Other Helpful Software for Quilt Design

Many quiltmakers enjoy using general-purpose drawing programs to design their quilts in addition to or in place of quilt designing software such as Electric Quilt or Quilt-Pro. Two popular programs are **Canvas by Deneba Software** (**http://www.deneba.com**) and **CorelDraw by Corel Corp.**(**http://www.corel.com**). Both are available for both PCs and Macs. You can download a trial of Canvas from Deneba's Web site. Here are more programs that will help you design quilts.

TESSELMANIA FROM KEVIN D. LEE
http://www.WorldOfEscher.com/store/mania.html

Create tessellating designs with this software available for both Macs and PCs.

GRAPHIC CONVERTER FROM LEMKE SOFTWARE
http://www.lemkesoft.de

A Mac program for fabric swatch scans for use in Quilt-Pro and other Mac graphics.

TRIANGLE ILLUSION FROM BURCIN KERMEN AND CENK GAZEN
http://www.cs.cmu.edu/afs/cs.cmu.edu/user/bcg/www/triangle/triangle.html

A Windows program for creating optical illusions on a triangular grid.

CREATIVE IMPULSE FROM ABCDESIGN
http://www.creativeimpulse.dk

Creative Impulse is software for creating arresting visual patterns. Head to the "Gallery" section of their Web site to see what we mean. The company is located in Denmark so the Web site may take a while to access.

GRAPH PAPER PRINTER FROM DR. PHILIPPE MARQUIS
http://perso.easynet.fr/~philimar/graphpapeng.htm

A free program for printing custom graph paper in any size or color.

GLIFTIC IMAGE GENERATOR FROM OWEN RANSEN
http://www.gliftic.com

Feeling uncreative? Select a color scheme, form, and interpretation, and this Windows program generates endless new ideas.

REPLIGATOR 6 FROM OWEN RANSEN
http://www.ransen.com/repligator/default.htm

Toss a traditional quilt block design into this Windows program and it will never be the same.

IRFANVIEW32 FROM IRFAN SKILJAN
http://stud4.tuwien.ac.at/~e9227474/main1.html

In order to use a scan of a fabric in one of the popular quilt design programs the image must be 256 colors or less. This free Windows program converts fabric images downloaded from the Internet (such as jpegs or gifs) to a 256-color bitmap. You can also apply special effects to your images and create a slideshow of your favorites.

▦ Web Sites With More Advice on Designing Quilts on a Computer

CARYL FALLERT TALKS ABOUT COMPUTERS AND QUILTING
http://www.bryerpatch.com/faq/computer.htm

Caryl answers questions like "How do you get the design from your computer onto a piece of paper as large as your quilt?" She also offers advice on designing quilts with CorelDraw.

DESIGN IDEAS FROM GLORIA HANSEN
http://www.gloriahansen.com

Head to "Design Ideas" for tutorials on playing with lines to create original quilt designs and scanning fabric for use as a fill pattern in Canvas.

!TIP *Run PC Quilt Design Software on a Mac* If you'd like to run Electric Quilt or other PC-only quilting software on your Macintosh, try **Virtual PC by Connectix** (**http://www.connectix.com/products/vpc.html**). It installs the Windows operating system of your choice on your Mac and allows you to easily toggle between the Mac and Windows OS.

!TIP *Never Get Lost on the Way to a Quilt Store Again* Have trouble navigating the roads of strange cities looking for some well-hidden museum or store? Plug your laptop into the nearest phone and tap into Vicinity Corp.'s **MapBlast** (**http://www.mapblast.com**). Type in the address of where you're located and the address to which you want to go and MapBlast will blast you a street map showing you how to get from point A to B. And it's free!

INDEX

ABOUT THE AUTHORS

Judy Heim

spends far too much time on the Internet printing patterns for quilts that she will never make. When she's not looking for more great sites on the Web, she writes books and magazine articles for a number of national publications. You can visit her on the Web at **http://www.catswhoquilt.com**.

Gloria Hansen

is the author of *Free Stuff for Traveling Quilters on the Internet* and the author or co-author of 12 other books. Gloria is also an award-winning quiltmaker who uses her Macintosh computers for quilt design. Gloria's quilts have appeared in numerous articles, books, and on television. Her quilts have been exhibited in many national and international shows. Gloria currently resides in East Windsor Township, New Jersey and is employed as a Web site designer and consultant. You can visit her Web site at: **http://www.gloriahansen.com**.

For more information on other fine books from C&T Publishing, write for a free catalog:
C&T Publishing, Inc., P.O. Box 1456, Lafayette, CA 94549
(800) 284-1114

http://www.ctpub.com
E-mail: ctinfo@ctpub.com

FREE STUFF ON THE INTERNET SERIES

Frustrated with spending hours of valuable time surfing your way around the Internet? C&T Publishing's Free Stuff on the Internet Series helps you quickly find information on your favorite craft or hobby. Our Free Stuff guides make it easy to stay organized as you visit hundreds of sites that offer all kinds of free patterns, articles, E-mail advice, galleries, and more. This series of handy guides lets you explore the Internet's infinite possibilities.

 PUBLISHING

www.ctpub.com